Without Walls

Without Walls

Walls

RANDY WHITE

Charisma
HOUSE
A STRANG COMPANY

WITHOUT WALLS by Randy White
Published by Charisma House
A Strang Company
600 Rinehart Road
Lake Mary, Florida 32746
www.charismahouse.com

Unless otherwise noted, all Scripture quotations are from the
King James Version of the Bible.

Scripture quotations marked NIV are from the Holy Bible, New
International Version. Copyright © 1973, 1978, 1984,
International Bible Society. Used by permission.

Incidents and persons portrayed in this volume are based on fact.
However, some names and details have been changed
to protect the privacy of individuals.

Library of Congress Cataloging-in-Publication Data
White, Randy, 1958-
Without walls: give me revival in my city or let me die! / by Randy
White.
p. cm.
ISBN 0-88419-564-3
1. Evangelistic work—Florida—Tampa—Case studies. 2. Without
Walls International church (Tampa, Fla.) I. Title.
BV3775.T36W47 1998
269'.2—dc21   98-41435
                                                         CIP

06 07 08 09 — 12 11 10 9 8
Printed in the United States of America

I LOVINGLY DEDICATE THIS BOOK TO:

My wife—Paula Michelle. You are my very best friend and closest confidante. You bring out the best in me and are the most tremendous helpmate God could have provided. You have worn so many hats and have played a variety of key, instrumental roles in helping to bring to pass the vision God placed in my heart. You are a woman after God's own heart, and I am so proud of you and the fire and passion you have for souls and for kingdom business.

*My parents—Frank and Darlene White—*who first instilled in me a love for souls and a zeal for Jesus.

*My children—Kristin, Angie, Brandon, and Bradley—*who are my never-ending source of joy, pleasure, and blessings.

*My staff and board at Without Walls International Church—*who are the best supporting cast a man could hope for—and tremendous armorbearers. No words can describe my gratitude and love.

*The members of Without Walls—*whose love, faithfulness, and commitment to the vision are cherished and absolutely invaluable.

*And lastly—*those who criticized, mocked, and did not believe in the vision. I thank you. You kept me on my knees. You kept me desperate for God to do the impossible. You kept me determined to do "thus saith the Lord." Jesus is always attracted to those who don't have enough.

ACKNOWLEDGMENTS

Grateful acknowledgment is given to the numerous contributors throughout my life and ministry, mentioned and unmentioned, who have poured into me, shaped me, and believed in the call of God on my life.

Myriads of people have encouraged me through the years by their example, vision, and lifestyle. My library is filled with incredible tapes and books that have changed my life and provided insight, wisdom, and revelation from historical men and women of God.

I am a student of Frances and Roland Long and Dr. T. L. Lowery. I thank God for my rich heritage—Bion Cecil, Bud Masser, Uncle Wayne Masser, and Daisy and T. L. Osborne—all of whom profoundly impact me today. Tommy Barnett, Rod Parsley, Bill Wilson, and T. D. Jakes provide me with standards of excellence by developing concepts and programs that have been mine to follow and duplicate.

Frances Long was my best encourager; she believed in me and prayed for me when everyone else had given up. She imparted the spirit of "giving it all" into my young life through her constant example.

I acknowledge those individuals who have given me suggestions and thoughts and helped me compile and put together this book. Jim Kerby, your time, efforts, and expressions are fabulous. I especially recognize and thank Jennifer Mallan, who always makes me shine.

I am indebted to Stephen and Joy Strang and Creation House for allowing me a publishing platform on which to share my vision and heartbeat with those who are hungry to win souls, reach the lost, meet the felt needs of the community, and heal hurts. There is a desperate need and cry for places of worship that have no walls—of tradition, religion, culture, economic status, or any other man-made remedy.

Most of all I would like to acknowledge my father and mother, Pastors Frank and Darlene White, innovators of programs that helped me get started in evangelism and restoration. My father had a coffee shop for the indigent and cut out the sides of a bus to do outdoor children's programs. Their imprint is on my life.

"Give me REVIVAL in my city, or let me die!"

CONTENTS

Welcome to Without Walls 1

Brokenness 11

Restoration 23

A Cloud by Day,
  a Fire by Night! 33

The Day of New Beginnings 39

Give Me Revival in This City,
  or Let Me Die! 45

If a Man Is Standing in the Rain,
  Give Him an Umbrella 49

How Much More Can God Call You? 57

The Vegetable-Soup Church 65

Don't Look Back! 71

Nothing Left but Ashes 77

Christmas Extravaganza 83

Does God Love Nobodies? 89

Do You See What I See? 93

Confounding the Church-
  Growth Experts 99

Healed of AIDS 105

Table in the Wilderness 109

If It Were Not for Without Walls,
  I'd Be Dead by Now 115

Sentenced to Church 119

Without Walls

If You Don't Put On a Program for Them,
  They'll Put On a Program for You! 123

The Easter Egg Hunt Miracle 127

Sitting Among Princes 131

Saved to the Uttermost 137

The Without Walls Ministry Team 143

I'm Going to Touch You As You've
  Never Been Touched 147

Heal the Sick in Body,
  Soul, and Spirit 151

Whatever Your Hands Find to Do 155

Let's Just Praise the Lord! 159

My Feet Are Firmly Planted 165

God Works in Mysterious Ways 169

A "Hand Up" Instead of a Handout 177

Victory Is Shouting in
  Our Neighborhood 181

So Send I You! 185

Persistence 191

The Student Teaches the Teacher 195

The Most Important
  Work I've Ever Done 199

Breaking the Curse 203

Fire! 207

The Power Pig 211

All I Know Is That He Loves Me 215

The God of the Valleys 221

The Need Is the Call 227

Contents

Treasures of the Heart 231

The Miracle Continues 237

The Harvest Is Ugly 241

The two key
principles for building
and growing the church
are evangelism and
restoration.
Both require focusing
on people outside the
walls of the sanctuary.

Welcome to
Without Walls

If you show up at Without Walls International Church just on Sunday morning, you'll miss most of the action.

Oh yes, we have a worship service, held for years in an inflatable tent we call the "Super Dome." The congregation sit in rows of white plastic lawn chairs, except when they are on their feet, arms raised to heaven, swept up in the glory of exuberant praise and worship. There's a choir too, with members of every age and color. One newspaper writer observed that "when the choir rocks on Sunday mornings, the dome's covering billows and expands, as if it had captured a hurricane."[1]

Preaching is a vital part of the Sunday morning service at our church. Most of the time I preach about evangelism and restoration, two of the key principles to building and growing a church. I believe every church should have a theme or vision that shapes its goals and outreaches and is continually emphasized to its membership. Too many churches have a new program every year—healing one year, the prophetic the next... they are a music church, a faith church, a Word church. For Without Walls, now and always, our theme is evangelism and restoration.

From the beginning, the Lord directed me to "preach to your congregation as if they were leaders." So instead of the service being a time of entertaining visitors with nice messages and music, I challenge the people before me to be leaders—evangelists, healers, counselors, witnesses, helpers. Each meeting is a time for celebration and instruction. Our people say they can't come to church and feel comfortable without being soulwinners. Jesus said:

> Heal the sick, cleanse the lepers, raise the dead, cast out devils: freely ye have received, freely give.
> —MATTHEW 10:8

So that's what we try to do.

I sometimes refer to our congregation as the "vegetable-soup" church because of the different ethnic, economic, racial, and social backgrounds. We have Asians, African Americans, Caucasians, South Africans, and Hispanics worshiping and working together. There are some of the wealthiest people in Florida's Hillsborough County sitting next to people living below the poverty line. We have those who have been prostitutes, drunkards, gang members, Mafia members, and homeless mixing with doctors, teachers, professional athletes, and top business leaders.

Often I ask the people to join hands as we pray together. "Feel that hand you are holding," I tell them. "Do you realize that hand is a miracle? You could be holding the hand of an ex-homosexual, ex-drug addict, ex-convict, ex-prostitute—all redeemed by Christ Jesus and washed clean by His blood!"

Once when I did this, I noticed three well-dressed ladies in the middle of the crowd. They let go of the hands of the strangers next to them, and by the time I finished praying, they were going out the door. Sadly, their action exemplifies the attitude of the typical church today.

Too many Christians allow their own fears and prejudices to limit who can be reached with the Good News of Jesus Christ. They recoil in disgust and horror at the people the apostle Paul described in 1 Corinthians 6:9–10: the fornicators, idolaters, adulterers, effeminate, abusers of themselves, thieves, covetous, drunk-ards, revilers, and extortioners. But they stop reading too soon. Verse 11 says, "And such were some of you." Thank God, the ground is level at the foot of the cross, and the blood of Jesus cleanses all people regardless of their background.

So the church *can* break down denominational walls, racial walls, and cultural walls. *It can be done!* When we get to heaven, we won't have assigned seats with those within our comfort zone or cultural background. We need to start getting along, loving, and helping each other down here on earth.

As pastor, it is my job to train and equip the people to go out and do the work of the ministry. That's how we became the church without walls.

PUTTING SNEAKERS ON THE GOSPEL

To really see our church in action, you'd have to go out on any afternoon with evangelism teams to Tampa's poorest areas—government housing projects like Rembrandt, College Hill, Oak Park Village, Central Park, North Boulevard, Robles Park, Blythe-Andrews, Kenneth Johnson, or Cutlas-Arms. The team members go door to door, talking to children and mothers, whoever will listen to them. They bring little gifts or treats, a colorful flyer, and an invitation to come out the next day when the big pink Operation Explosion truck rolls in for a great show. Some folks are suspicious and afraid, a few belligerent and menacing, but most are open and receptive.

The next day when the rolling sanctuary pulls into the inner-city field or parking lot, kids run after it like the Pied Piper. Dropping the folding sides down to reveal a brightly decorated sound stage, an energetic cast of clowns and other performers begin a one-hour dynamic, action-packed program. There are balloons, music, flags, costumed characters, crazy stage games, and contests. There are skits teaching simple lessons about staying in school and away from trouble, and simple but intense messages on the basic values of life...and about a loving God who knows and cares about each individual.

Without Walls

Two hundred or more kids may show up to be loved, hugged, and encouraged at each stop the big pink trucks make at ten different housing projects. These portable hope stations beam the light of God's love to sixteen hundred to twenty-four hundred children each week.

You might also see Without Walls in action at the Operation Med-Care Center, located in a reconditioned four-story office building. Babies needing immunizations, single mothers with sick children, elderly people with no one to help them, the homeless, all kinds of people who have fallen through the cracks of government health care programs come to see a board-certified physician at the clinic. With Medicaid being canceled and welfare money phasing out, increasing numbers of sick, hurting, and frightened people are being ministered to in love. They respond gratefully to reassuring words, a compassionate touch, and a whispered prayer. The medical center also has a van pickup service to bring people to see the doctors, as well as a rolling medical center that visits the heart of the inner city to treat hundreds of shut-ins who have no one else to turn to for help.

Monday through Friday, kids with special educational needs and learning disorders show up at a specialized academy. The last thing we wanted to do was create another Christian school. But we soon discovered that as many as 80 percent of the children living in public housing have been labeled as hyperactive, ADD (attention deficit disorder), SLD (slow learning disorder), or some other educational or behavioral "disability." Inner-city youngsters are commonly drugged with Ritalin, depressants, or other medications to combat their disruptive "conditions." Using individual learning stations and special curricula, students learn at their own pace, with personalized attention from qualified instructors. Often a student will master three or four grade levels in a single term at the academy. Our special school accepts kids with these problems who are not being taught anything in public school except how to fail again.

Bob, at age fourteen, could not read or spell—not even c-a-t or g-o! Each of his six siblings had a different father. His mother's lifestyle had been a great hindrance to a stable, ready-to-learn environment. After several months in our program, he mastered the ABCs, learned a basic word vocabulary, some phonics, and could read simple sentences.

Jonette came to Without Walls while under "house arrest" for throwing acid in another girl's face. In jail she heard the gospel, and she accepted Christ. But with her highly publicized record, no school would accept her. As a volunteer worker at Without Walls, she tearfully asked for a chance to learn. In the academy, she excelled in every subject and won fifteen trophies for outstanding achievement and exemplary citizenship. In addition to tutoring younger students, she also served as the physical education instructor.

Antoine had a long-standing pattern of failure and believed the public school's assessment that he was not capable of learning basic skills. Yet he was quick and bright in picking up common-sense tasks and skills. In two years, he progressed from a fourth-grade math level and second-grade reading and spelling skills to solid eighth-grade performance in all areas.

Down the hall, classes are going on for Destiny Bible College, a full-fledged, in-depth study program for people who feel they have a call of God on their lives and are interested in preparing themselves for ministry. In our first two years when 80 percent of our members were first-generation new converts, we taught basic Bible concepts and spiritual principles—what it means to be a Christian. On the next floor down, a qualified specialist conducts a financial counseling session for members of the congregation with money and credit problems. And in another classroom, a dozen or so men and women pore over workbooks designed to help prepare them to take the GED (General Education Development) test and receive a high-school equivalency certificate. This program is sponsored by the state and receives government funding to enable virtually any student to be able to attend.

Outside on the parking lot, several guys huddle around and climb in and out of three semitrailer trucks, backing up, pulling forward, driving out into the surrounding streets. They are involved in the vo-tech/trade education program, specifically the truck driving school and state-certified testing program. Several blocks away, women enrolled in our cosmetology school are getting hands-on training in skin care, makeup, nail sculpting, and hairdressing. A job placement service is available when they're ready to go to work.

Perhaps you'd be interested in attending the Friday morning Corporate Evangelical Outreach (CEO) meeting—a bimonthly Bible study conducted by, and for, business and professional men and women in Tampa. The gospel is just as needed and just as effective for "up-and-outers" as for "down-and-outers."

Quietly, almost behind the scenes, witnesses from Without Walls minister each week to patients in nursing and convalescent homes through praise and worship services, one-on-one visitation, and prayer. These are the forgotten citizens, those who cannot get out to attend church. So we take church to them.

Each Saturday morning at eight o'clock, volunteers armed with a vision and a complete breakfast head for various locations within the city to feed—physically and spiritually—hundreds of Tampa's homeless people on park benches, under bridges, in cardboard box "parks," and labor pools. Some are fugitives, vagabonds, mentally disabled...others are just temporarily down on their luck. There are men and women, sometimes entire families, old and young, from all areas and circumstances. On Sunday morning, these friends are transported to church for the morning service. After the service they are provided a complete meal, and someone discusses their situation with them. Whether they need clothing or counseling, medical care or a job lead, our members try to provide the help needed to get these people on the road to recovery.

While you were checking out these ministries, you didn't get the chance to drop in on the Monday night Women of the Word Bible study, the Angels of Love outreach to the terminally ill, the adoption support group, or the foster care training program. And you may also have missed dropping by the Pregnancy Crisis Center or observing a rehearsal of the church drama team. What about the prison ministry outreach, or the Liberty Ministries meeting with members of the homosexual community, or this week's session of the X-Strippers Support Network?

Other programs operated by Without Walls include a day-care

center, a teen rock-music club, a training course to help people get off welfare (in 1997, three hundred mothers in our program became self-sufficient), and a community food pantry and clothes closet. There are more than two hundred outreach ministries to various segments and areas of the community.

Has anyone told you about Without Walls' special events ministries, which include an annual Easter egg hunt (they exceeded the *Guinness Book of World Records* of 119,00 eggs by having more than 300,000 eggs), a Christmas toy giveaway that provides forty thousand toys to families in need, and a Back-to-School Bash that provides school supplies, haircuts, physicals, and food for underprivileged children from government housing projects? There is also an annual "Table in the Wilderness," which feeds thousands of homeless and hungry people the day after Thanksgiving. A recent New Year's Eve celebration featured converted rapper M. C. Hammer, Christian soul-singer Denise Smith, and BeBe Winans and family. Church at Without Walls is never boring.

Since 1991, Without Walls' annual budget has grown from three hundred thousand dollars to six million dollars, more than half of which comes from donations outside the congregation. But the real assets of the church are the people who have caught the vision and provide the hands-on involvement that enables the church to reach "outside the walls" of the church into the community.

Without Walls exists because of people like...

> ...*Kevin,* who is part of the Loyal Warriors Motorcycle Ministry. Kevin gets his paycheck from the maintenance department of a downtown Tampa office, but his real work is done astride his Harley-Davidson. He goes to rallies, schools, outdoor concerts—wherever his bike takes him. "It gets me in the door," he says of his motorcycle, "and it helps me reach an audience not accustomed to hearing the Word of God. Riding is what I know best, and I'm using it to serve the Lord."

> ...*John and Diane,* who found personal fulfillment at the church. Diane was just glad to get her reluctant husband to come to church with her. He hadn't been to church in nearly

thirty years, and Diane had "bugged" him about it so long that he finally agreed to go for a half hour just to get her off his back. When the half hour was over, John decided to stay—and has been there ever since! John was won over by seeing Christians who didn't just talk about their faith, but they rolled up their sleeves and put their faith into action. John says, "The idea of a working church made sense to me—this was 100 percent genuine Christianity, touching, lifting, helping, making a difference. I wanted to be a part of something this real." The bulletin that first Sunday morning included a small notice that a photographer was needed to take pictures of church guests and other church-related activities. A commercial photographer, John volunteered his services. John now attends Destiny Bible College, and he and Diane serve on the welcoming committee for newcomers. As a bonus, they say their involvement in the ministry of Without Walls has dramatically improved their marriage.

... *Wanda*, a health-care professional who loves the unlimited opportunities for service at Without Walls. "There are churches where the pastor says, 'This is what you can do if you work within the confines of my ministry,'" says Wanda. "But Pastors Randy and Paula White say, 'Make use of the gifts God has given you, and go for it!'"

TWO THOUSAND ON SUNDAY— TEN THOUSAND DURING THE WEEK

You can't possibly see everything that goes on in any given week at Without Walls International Church. Besides the "usual" programs like graded Sunday school classes; children, youth, and single's activity groups; nurseries; men and women's ministries; and prayer meetings, the real work of making an impact on our city takes place out where the needs are. The two thousand who attend Sunday services will go out into the highways and hedges and touch the lives of ten thousand more during the week.

Since Without Walls was founded in 1991, our ministry teams

have been targeting the toughest, neediest areas in the city of Tampa—the inner-city public housing projects. In 1998, the press reported that for the first time ever the crime rate dropped—by a whopping 14 percent. Could our efforts have contributed to this double-digit decrease? I believe we had to have an effect, and evidently the public housing authorities agree. They're requesting that we put our Operation Explosion program to work in all the city's project locations.

The Juvenile Detention Center has invited us to conduct Bible studies in their facilities. The public school system repeatedly praises the work of our Conquering Force team of strongmen who, sponsored by secular agencies, invade campuses during school hours to present programs emphasizing staying in school and avoiding trouble, all with strong Christian testimonies.

Politicians call on us to help them find answers for civic problems. We're invited to offer input at city council meetings. Civic leaders and groups are generous with accolades and endorsements. In 1996, the mayor's office presented us with a key to the city, an honor usually reserved for visiting foreign ambassadors, high-level dignitaries, and highly affluent and influential citizens.

While we've never sought honor, position, or awards, we are receiving recognition as we concentrate on doing what God called us to do.

Our mission and purpose is simple—very basic: We want everybody in our city to know Jesus Christ! The only way that can happen is through evangelism and restoration. It's a big goal, but we're giving it our best.

---

1. Michelle Bearden, "Worship Without Walls," *The Tampa Tribune,* 17 December 1997.

The church is full of people with skeletons in their closets.

Brokenness

I dumped a beat-up old suitcase and a couple of paper sacks into the back of the car—all the material possessions I owned in the world. When I slammed the trunk of my 1966 Ford Mustang, thin shards of rust shook loose from underneath and showered down on the dusty pavement.

Suddenly overcome by emotion, I sat down on the curb behind the car and sobbed like a child. In a matter of weeks, my life had been totally shattered. My ministry, position, ambitions, and dreams had been smashed. My finances were in shambles. My marriage and family life were broken and ruined. Everything I ever held dear in my whole life had been taken away.

Worse still, my relationship with God had been interrupted. The Spirit and presence of the Lord that had seemed so close and natural to me had somehow slipped away, and I felt only emptiness inside. When had the mantle of God's holy anointing—that which had become the single most important thing I lived for—been lifted from me? When did it go? I couldn't remember.

Everything seemed confused and dark. I felt a heaviness that nearly crushed my chest and an ominous foreboding that made my heart pound so that I could never rest. No matter how I tried, I couldn't sort out the tattered, tangled debris of my life enough even to assess my situation.

For years I'd known there were desperate problems, but I just couldn't hold things together. Knowing that an inescapable storm was bearing down on me, I tried to tape the windows, pile up the sandbags, and board up my life to protect it from the oncoming wind and rain. Then, without warning, a massive tidal wave swept over me and washed away everything. It was far more destructive and terrible than I'd even dared to imagine.

Sitting alone on the curb behind that worn-out old car, my mind grieved over every loss and whirled with desperate questions. Where would I go? What would I do? Was I mistaken about the call of God on my life? Were the promises—the vision I believed He had given me—really true? But there were no answers, and after a while I ran out of tears again.

Finally, in the awful exhaustion that comes only with total despair, I looked up into the sky and, in an audible voice, asked one last question of a holy God—"What now?"

Many great Christians have told of hearing the voice of God. I have no doubt that He may sometimes speak audibly. But I am also convinced that His voice may even sound louder when He speaks to a person's inner being. That's what happened to me that day as the Lord God spoke to my spirit and said, "Now that there's nothing left, I'll prove to you that I am God, and I will restore everything to you."

The process of restoration in my life had begun. And without that word from the Lord, I honestly don't think I could have gone on.

WHERE I CAME FROM

I had been brought up in a full-gospel pastor's home. As early as age thirteen, I began to get involved in the ministry of my father's church. I worked in the church's coffeehouse, went on prison ministry trips, and preached on the streets and in the parks. Even then, the principles of how to have a church without walls were being formed in my heart.

But like many teenagers who are brought up in Christian homes, I had a period of restlessness when I sometimes had a rebellious attitude toward God and my parents. It seemed to me at the time that I was always hearing "You can't do that!" or "We don't believe in that!" I couldn't go swimming or bowling. I couldn't go to the movies. I couldn't go to my high school prom. I couldn't do this or do that. Sometimes I felt that our church knew what we didn't believe more than what we did believe! I chafed under those restraints and decided to find a way to get away from the legalism of the church.

So when I was only seventeen, I met a girl and decided to get married. She was a nice girl from a good home, but she was not from my full-gospel background. She didn't understand what being "called to the ministry" meant to me. Without any advice from anyone, with no premarital counseling, no prayer or planning, she and I got married. I immediately took her away from her family, and we went off to Lee College.

I had graduated after my junior year in high school—all I had to do was take an English class in summer school. Then I enrolled in college. I thought I had life all figured out. I knew quite a bit about the ministry and had some talent for Christian service. I was clever enough to figure out how things worked and to take advantage of every opportunity. And by getting married, I'd found a way to be out from under the direction of my church and my family and to be on my own. Back then I was supremely confident that I had all the answers.

Although I was mildly rebellious against what I thought was the church's emphasis on petty things, I loved God and the work of the church. In my heart of hearts, I treasured my personal relationship with the Lord. I'd never considered doing anything but becoming a gospel preacher like my father. With her non-church background, my new wife had little understanding or appreciation for my church's distinctive protocol, and she didn't share my passion and zeal—my total immersion into the work of the ministry.

From that beginning point, we steadily grew even further apart.

Without Walls

For the first few years when we were having our three children, we managed to get along okay, mainly because she was so devoted and involved with our two daughters, Angie and Kristin, and our son, Brandon. I gave her little of my time or attention, giving my studies and ministry activities top priority. There was no balance in my life.

After college I was assigned to a small, struggling church with lots of problems. In my zeal to succeed as a minister, I worked as if I were driven, going almost night and day. But the congregation's difficulties were resolved, and the church's growth broke all attendance records in my state.

Then I became an associate minister with Dr. T. L. Lowery, one of the leading pastors in the denomination, with a very large and prestigious congregation. I became a spokesman for Christian causes within my home community, achieving high visibility and media recognition. I also started traveling a great deal as an evangelist, enjoying tremendous success. I spoke somewhere almost every night, and was booked up for two years in advance. Two pilot friends flew me from meeting to meeting, lending me their planes at no charge.

The more successful I became in the ministry, the more my marriage and my family suffered. I was gone much of the time, and I was totally absorbed by church work when I was in town. My wife couldn't travel at my hectic pace with young children, so I was guilty of just not including her in my world. Somehow I had the mistaken notion that since I was spending all my time working for the Lord, He would take care of my family.

I was doing very well financially, so I bought a couple of businesses and found someone to operate them for me. I had a limousine service and an appliance business. Then I was offered a management position with a company that operated thirty homes for the indigent. I could handle my responsibilities there and still work in the church and go out on speaking engagements. By then I had a six-figure income and enjoyed the accolades of my associates and my church. Articles about my activities were appearing in national Christian publications.

I was still young and green and naively thought I knew it all. I assumed that success was always going to be easy. Almost all of my ministry goals were being accomplished, it seemed, and I was enjoying the recognition I was getting.

But things weren't going well at home. My relationship with my wife was getting more and more strained and troubled. I spent so little time with her; I expected her to handle everything at home and make her life accommodate my plans and schedule. It was so unfair to her. Looking back now, I can see that I sure wouldn't have wanted to be married to me! And I sure wouldn't have wanted a husband like me for my daughters.

But by the time I realized how seriously our marriage had deteriorated, I had so many commitments on my time that I didn't know how to get myself loose. And we'd grown so far apart that perhaps neither of us knew how to find our way back. Our situation was bad and steadily getting worse.

Nevertheless, I insisted that we had to make our marriage work. In my world, divorce was not an option. Marriage was forever, "till death do you part." The rules of the church were very clear that divorced people had no place in ministry.

So we endured a troubled marriage for thirteen years. We tried to make the best of a bad situation. The greatest blessings and joy we shared were our three beautiful children. Despite the problems in our marriage, I loved my children and was so proud of them. And with each passing year, my relationship with Angie, Kristin, and Brandon becomes more enriching and important to me.

I was guilty not only of neglecting the responsibilities of my marriage and my family, but of allowing the politics and mechanics of ministry to take precedence over my relationship with God. I believe when Christians experience failure, it is because of what they choose to do instead of following God's agenda for them. My priorities have been radically changed. Now my relationship to God, to my wife, and to my family always comes before activities and things.

But not then. And eventually my wife couldn't take any more and gave up on the marriage. I was miserable, too. We separated and came to realize that our differences really were irreconcilable.

Without Walls

Divorce... and Desolation

After wrestling with the inevitable for months, like a condemned man taking his last walk to the execution chamber, we headed for divorce. And because the terms were uncontested, the legalities proceeded quickly. Soon the devastating deed was done, the notices published. And the news spread.

I no longer could be the associate pastor of the great church where my senior pastor was "grooming me to take over." I was no longer welcomed as an evangelist in all the churches across the nation where I had been scheduled. How could I go and minister to others when my own life was out of order? In fact, there was no place in my church association where I, as a divorced person, could officially function in any position of authority.

I left the house and furnishings to my ex-wife and my children, and I signed over the limo business as a source of income for them. I relinquished my position with the company that provided homes for the indigent and let the appliance business—which was struggling without strong leadership—just wind down. The businesses had never been important to me—they were just byproducts of the blessing of God. Now that my ministry was seemingly finished, life was empty and bitter.

Within a matter of weeks, everything was gone. I was totally devastated. Everything I owned would fit into the trunk of that beat-up old '66 Mustang. With no place else to go, I moved back into my folk's house. I thought my life was over.

Then came that fateful day when I heard the voice of God. I was so broken and down that I could barely hope, much less believe. So I just hung on and waited to see what would happen.

I got a secular job as an engineer for the State Department in Washington, D.C., about twenty miles from the church where I had worked. It was a great job, but after working for the Lord most of my life, I found it dull and unfulfilling. But it gave me something to do with my time, and it provided an income.

Then my pastor, Dr. T. L. Lowery, began ministering to me. He actually helped see me through the aftermath of the divorce and helped me start getting up from where I had fallen. I had been knocked down, he told me, but it was time to again stand up on my feet.

That man of God took hours from his crowded schedule to counsel and pray with me. "God still loves you and wants to use you," he said. "There is hope for you."

Little by little, he brought me back to work with him. I wasn't on staff. I didn't have an official, permanent position. Everything I did was on a volunteer basis. Sometimes I just worked around the building, doing maintenance, cleaning, being a janitor. I painted the boiler room, mowed the grass, set up chairs. It didn't matter to me—I was back doing something for the Lord!

After a while, I got the chance to do visitation, then work with the bus ministry. Slowly, deliberately, I worked my way back into the ministry.

THE WAY BACK

It was different this time. The emphasis wasn't on me but on the people I could serve. I wasn't in the spotlight—there was very little glory or recognition for what I was doing. But every day I said, "Thank You, Lord, for letting me work for You!"

Finally, after a year and a half or more, Dr. Lowery offered me a full-time position on his staff. I refused it because I knew it would cause him trouble and bring reproach on his ministry. Then he offered me a job with his church school. I turned that down, too.

I was beginning to preach again at my dad's church. "You're my son, and my people know what you've been through. It will be okay," he told me. And it was. Standing in the pulpit and ministering the Word of God was a tremendous healing process. The first time I felt that indescribable sensation of the anointing of the Holy Spirit stirring inside my heart again, tears poured from my eyes and wet my whole face!

Then I began to travel again with Dr. Lowery, going along to drive for him and to help put up the tent. Then I began doing some light ministry—making the announcements, speaking in the afternoon service. What a joy to be preaching again!

"You're going to make it, Randy," he said. "The anointing of God is still on you. The Lord still has a work for you to do!"

One night I preached at my dad's church. After the service a striking, young blonde woman named Paula came up to me. She'd heard that I'd had considerable business experience and wondered if we could have lunch together so she could get some advice on her business. She was going through the pain of a divorce and was putting together a housecleaning service to help support herself and her son, Bradley.

We went to lunch, although I'm not sure how much business we really discussed. We liked each other and had a pleasant discussion together. We had some things in common—I'd been deeply hurt as a result of my divorce, and Paula had been very wounded, too. Both of us were desperately trying to hear from God and find a way to rebuild our lives.

I learned that Paula had endured many tragic experiences. Although outwardly self-assured, she was very broken inwardly. Her father had committed suicide when she was five, and she'd been sexually and physically abused in her childhood. She'd had a teenage pregnancy and a bad marriage. She had some major scars—and a tremendous hunger for God.

Very slowly, very tentatively, we began to see each other. We were both eager to work for the Lord. A relatively new Christian, Paula was completely sold out to God, totally enthusiastic about finding ways to serve Him. This was tremendously attractive to me—for that was my passion as well.

After dating for several months, I think we both felt that what was happening was too good to be true. Neither of us really felt deserving of such good fortune. Although desperate for a second chance at happiness, we were even more concerned about being in God's perfect will. We didn't want our relationship—that of two divorced individuals—to be a stumbling block to others, in or out of the church.

We actually broke off our relationship for a few months as we prayed and sought God's direction. Should we seek reconciliation with our ex-spouses? It was a torturous struggle. I lost forty pounds during this time of intense emotional agonizing and soul-searching. Eventually we both realized we could never go back and change the past. We had to start over.

We began working together on some ministry projects at my dad's church. She had worked in the nursery, then with the preschoolers and teens. She was dynamic and fun, and she got tremendous results.

THE PRECIOUS GIFT OF A SECOND CHANCE

Paula and I started a bus ministry together and built it into a strong and productive outreach. We both had a heart for the poor and the underdog. On Thanksgiving, unable to get any significant funding for a holiday meal for the poor, we pooled our money and bought some turkeys. Paula cooked them, and we prepared bag lunches. We took them to downtown Washington, D.C., and handed them out to the street people.

I've never had so much fun. That day, serving the poor and homeless with food we had paid for ourselves, we laughed and had the best time, reveling in the joy of the Lord together. I think we both began to realize that we had found our soul mate!

After we'd dated for about a year, we went on a tour to Israel with a group from Dr. Lowery's church where we worked part time. I'd told him that I intended to ask Paula to marry me on the trip. He was delighted!

We'd arranged to take a midnight cruise on the Sea of Galilee, perhaps the most beautiful spot in all of Israel. I'd asked the captain of the ship to stop the engines at the stroke of midnight. Paula and I were standing together, watching the moon's reflection in the sparkling water when the throbbing engine fell silent, and the boat slipped silently along.

I got on my knees, took Paula's hands in mine, and asked her to marry me and join me in working for the Lord for the rest of our lives. I told her I loved her and asked her to please say yes. It was very romantic.

And she did say yes!

We were married about six months later. It was a beautiful ceremony. We both were so grateful to God to be starting a new life and a new ministry together, and we were very determined not to allow the mistakes and failures of the past to be repeated.

Paula and I have a very strong marriage. We know about the devastation of divorce and the many pitfalls that can threaten a marriage. We try to play as hard as we work! No matter how busy our schedule, we make time to spend alone together at least twice each week. I have had the privilege of becoming "Dad" to Paula's son, Bradley. If we're out of town, we communicate. We work hard to maintain a tremendous trust factor with each other. Our first responsibility is to each other.

I've maintained a close relationship with my children over the years, and they love Paula. My middle daughter, Angie, came to live with us when she went to college at the University of South Florida.

God is so good to us. Why do I sleep, eat, preach, and live the message of restoration? It is because I was the prime candidate and recipient of an abundant amount of grace!

We must get rid of the "Kleenex mentality" and stop trying to throw away people who are messed up and dirty. The central truth of the Bible is—"He restoreth my soul . . ." (Ps. 23:3).

Restoration

The Twenty-third Psalm is so rich in truth that a separate sermon could be preached—and probably has been—on each verse. But I think the key to the whole chapter—indeed, the central truth of the entire Bible—is in verse 3: "He restoreth my soul..."

Jesus restores everything the enemy has taken from you—your family, your finances, your hope, your ministry, your joy, your peace of mind—everything. You have never gone too far, sunk too low, or gotten so lost that He cannot find you and bring you back. And you have never messed up so bad that He can't restore you. Regardless of your offense, He forgives. No matter how much you have ruined and wasted, He will give back "exceeding abundantly above all that we ask or think" (Eph. 3:20). When we give Him our brokenness and strife, He turns it around and makes our life into something beautiful.

Jesus is our Restorer! This church has been grounded upon the principle of restoration. Our mission is to evangelize all of this city and to restore every person who comes to us broken.

Our God is a God of restoration. Judges 16 tells the story of

Samson, who messed up so miserably. Verse 22 says, "Howbeit the hair of his head began to grow again.....". God did not reject him; Samson's strength was restored.

Jonah 3:1 conveys a story of restoration: "And the word of the LORD came unto Jonah the second time...."

Genesis 28 tells how Jacob, after stealing his brother's birthright, went to a place called Bethel, where he had an encounter with God.

Saul the Pharisee became Paul the Apostle, who declared, "Therefore if any man be in Christ, he is a new creature: old things are passed away; behold, all things are become new" (2 Cor. 5:17). Paul knew about restoration.

DAVID'S STORY

David, the writer of the Twenty-third Psalm, is one of my favorite characters in the Bible. God said, "This man, David, has My heart. He doesn't always do things right—he's always messing up—but he has My heart."

What comes to your mind when you think of David? He was a musician who wrote songs to God that are so good they would be on the Top Ten list if he were alive today. He was a prophet, amazingly used to proclaim God's message to the people of his day and to all generations.

I envision David as a little red-headed, freckle-faced boy sitting on a creek bank watching over his sheep, and playing on a harp. I think of David the fighter who killed a lion and a bear, and who went up against a thirteen-foot giant with only a slingshot. I think of David, anointed to be king. I think of David, the saint who loved God with all his heart.

But if I read the entire Bible record, I also have to think of David the sinner, David the lousy husband, David the schemer, David the murderer. God didn't hide the faults, failures, mistakes, and backslidings of David, or those of other great men of the Bible. He wants us to know that it doesn't take a perfect person, a champion, or a superhero to follow Him and to do His will. So He tells the whole story of all these men—the good and the bad.

But He doesn't leave them in their collapses, their failures, their falls from grace. God is a restorer.

There are times when I look in the mirror and see somebody I don't like. Sometimes I see someone that nobody likes! There are times I look in the mirror and wonder if I'm saved. Some mornings when I get up, I feel that I need to call a taxi to get from the bedroom to the bathroom. Those are the times when I want to turn off the lights, take the phone off the hook, and pull the covers over my head. Have you ever felt that way?

I believe David had some mornings like that. He was no novice. He was a theologian and a sinner...a singer and an adulterer...a king and a murderer. He knew what it was like to have friends betray him, to have rebellious children and a dysfunctional family. He knew what it was to taste war up close and personal. He knew the sickening, guilty, sinking feeling of being a sinner. I know that when he looked at his mistakes and failures, he must have thought, *I don't want to live anymore.* He knew what it was like to live life at its best and its worst.

So it really means something when David writes, "He restoreth my soul."

We live in a throwaway society. You might say we have a "Kleenex mentality"—if it's messed up, throw it away. We don't save much of anything—clothes, furniture, cars, whatever. Use it and lose it. If it's not right, get rid of it.

Sadly, that disposable attitude carries over into human relations as well. Marriage not working? Junk it. Pregnancy inconvenient? Abort it. Mentally ill people hard to help and treat? Dump them on the streets. Family members causing trouble? Throw them out. Friends in trouble and becoming a drag? Say "so long" and move on.

But David says, "Listen, when God sees you, He doesn't throw up His hands and turn His back. He lifts you up, brings you back, and restores you."

DEAD BATTERIES CAN BE RECHARGED!

I attended Lee College in Cleveland, Tennessee, right out of high school. I was seventeen years old. That's when I discovered what it means to be poor. I had no regular income, just what I could pick up doing odd jobs between classes and studying. I had to pay seventy-five dollars a month to live in a house trailer up on a hill.

Living off campus, I needed transportation back and forth to class. But I couldn't afford a real car. All I had was a 1972 Vega with a five-speed manual transmission. Now, the guy who invented the Vega should have been shot because of all the grief he caused the owners of those vehicles. The Vega engine had an aluminum block, and when it got hot it would expand, allowing oil to seep around the steel cylinders and go through and foul the plugs. When you pulled up to a stop light and looked back, there was a big blue cloud of smoke coming out the tailpipe and following along behind.

I don't know much about cars. All I really knew was that the Vega looked pretty good, but it would hardly ever run. Then it got to where it wouldn't start. I went out to drive to class, turned the key, and it just went chuh...ch...ch...ch. Dead battery.

Well, I got someone to push me and get the car rolling down the hill. Then I shifted into third gear, popped the clutch, and it started right up. I'd drive to class and park where I knew I could push it out into the street later. If I had to go anywhere else besides school or home, I'd have to park the car on a level spot, pull the emergency brake, and leave it running until I got back. Once I turned off the engine, I couldn't get it started again without pushing the car.

One time there was no one to help me get the car started. I put the transmission in a high gear, aimed the car down the hill, went behind and pushed it myself. I gave one big shove, and the Vega started and took off down the hill, with nobody driving. I nearly killed myself running to catch up and pull myself inside.

About now you're wondering, "Why didn't you just get a new battery?" Are you serious? At that time, a battery for that car cost about thirty dollars. To me, a seventeen-year-old college student with no steady income and a wife to support, that seemed like three hundred thousand dollars. I mean, I was buying bags of leftover donuts for a quarter, and we were eating those stale delicacies all week long. I bought gasoline for that car fifty cents and a dollar at a time.

But then I heard from home and learned that my mom and dad were coming for a visit. Oh, joy! Dad would be my savior and write me a check. I'd eat some real food when he got there. He'd buy me a new battery for that old car.

So when my parents arrived, right away I told my father that the battery was dead in my car and needed to be replaced. I'd been pushing the car to start it for months. "Before we go and get a new one, let me look at that battery," he said.

In just two or three minutes he came back, wiping grease off his hands with an old rag, and shaking his head. I thought, *Maybe the battery cables were loose, and he just had to tighten up the clamps on the terminals.*

Then Dad explained it to me, and his words of wisdom still ring in my ears to this day. What profound insight, delivered with such genuine passion. "You idiot!" he said. "There's no water in the battery." He got a can of water and filled up all the cells in the battery. Then we pushed the car to start it, let it run for a while, and turned off the key. "Now try to start it," he said.

When I twisted that key again, the starter turned and the engine roared back to life. "Well, what do you know," I said lamely, "it works!" As it turned out, that battery ended up outlasting the car.

There's an important spiritual application to this story. I had the wrong concept and wanted to throw away the trouble. But my dad said, "Batteries can come back even after they're totally run down."

The old battery had no power left. It didn't do what it was supposed to do. The only solution I could see was to ditch it and get a new one to take its place. But my father said, "No, let's give the old battery another chance. Let's give it a drink of fresh water. Let's put some power back in it and recharge it. Let's just look after it for a little while and see what happens."

Yes, that was the battery that had let me down. It had quit on me, inconvenienced me, aggravated me, disappointed me. But with the touch of my father's hand, pretty soon that battery was restored and ready to work again. It was ready to be productive. And in no time at all, I started depending on it and trusting it again. Do you get the picture?

Without Walls

SHARPENING THE CUTTING EDGE

Another time I learned a lesson about restoration. I had moved from the house trailer on the hill in Cleveland, Tennessee, to a place called South Street in Frederick, Maryland. It was literally on the other side of the railroad tracks, a stone's throw from the inner city.

My financial situation hadn't improved a great deal—I was still scraping to get by. I decided I was going to stay warm that winter by burning wood. Somebody had given me an old pot belly stove, so all I needed was some firewood.

Then a man came by in a truck with a load of green hickory scrap wood, and I talked him into giving it to me. "You don't want this stuff," he said.

"Yes, I do," I replied. "I'm going to cut it up and burn it."

I'd watched my father cut wood when I was younger. He'd take an ax and start chopping and splitting, and in a few hours he had a big pile of firewood. It looked pretty easy to me.

So I borrowed a brand-new ax from my neighbor and went out to chop up that green hickory. I raised that ax over my head, took a big swing, and hit my first hickory limb. Bam! That ax bounced back and nearly took my head off.

I hit it again...and again. There was barely a dent in the limb. Every time I swung the ax, it just bounced off that green wood. I got mad and made up my mind that I was not going to be defeated. I hit that limb up on a block. I hit it down the sidewalk. I hit it underneath the fence and down the cellar steps. I hit that wood every direction it was possible to hit it. But it never did cut.

The ax, on the other hand, looked as if it had been in Mount St. Helen's volcano. It was dented, chipped, and dull—it looked thirty years old. I thought, *My neighbor is going to kill me when he sees what I've done to his brand-new ax.*

Sure enough, a week or so later he knocked on my door and wanted his ax back. I was too embarrassed to even go get it for him. I just mumbled, "It's down in the cellar."

About an hour later, I heard him chopping. I peeked out, and he was cutting wood, the chips flying everywhere. How could that be? I had to go see.

When he stopped to rest a minute, I asked, "How do you do that? I know that ax was dull."

"Oh," he said, "I took it back to the hardware store, and they sharpened it for me. They put it on the grinder and gave it a new edge. Then I got me some seasoned oak logs, and it's cutting just fine."

The psalmist David said, "Through the storms and setbacks and mistakes, I've been dulled and nicked. I've been scarred until I lost my effectiveness. But God put me back on the wheel and restored the fresh, sharp, cutting edge of my life."

FINISHED . . . OR REFINISHED?

My Uncle Wayne once gave me a bed. Now, that was something for him because he had a reputation of being really tight with his money and possessions. Uncle Wayne was a collector—he bought and sold various items he picked up or traded for.

One day I flagged him down as he was driving past in his old truck. He was hauling a load of junk from the barn to the dump. If Uncle Wayne was throwing something away, it really had to be in bad shape.

He had an old wooden bedframe on the truck, and it did look rough. It had been painted with enamel paint four or five times, and it was matted with straw and pigeon dung from the barn. "Maybe I could use this," I said. "I need a bed."

"You can have it if you want," he said, "but it's all broken down and in bad shape." And he gave it to me, which I thought was a miracle.

I loaded the bed in my truck and took it to a man who refinished and restored furniture. I thought maybe he could clean it up and repaint it so I could use it. When I went back to get it, I couldn't believe my eyes. There was a beautiful oak bed, with the natural grain showing; it just glistened and shone. The headboard had a carving of a sea captain at the helm of a ship. It was beautiful.

"Are you sure this is the same bed?" I asked. The man explained that he didn't try to cover up the filth and grime on that piece of furniture; instead, he scrubbed off all the dirt and old paint. He stripped it to the bare wood, down to the original design. Then he repaired the broken sections, skillfully making the frame as good as new. Finally he put on several coats of wood finish to beautify and protect it. Everyone who saw that old bed was amazed at how beautiful and valuable it was after it had been restored.

David was saying in the Twenty-third Psalm, "The God that I serve looked beyond the dinginess of my life—saw right through the cover-ups—and recognized the original beauty underneath. He saw through my facade, where I told everybody I was doing fine, where I whistled and sang on the outside. He saw me hiding in shame and sorrow, heard me crying myself to sleep. And He took me gently in His hands and stripped away all the dirty rags I was wrapped in, washing away the grime and dirt until my original design and purpose were revealed once more. Then He anointed me with oil, dressed me in new clothes, and sent me out with a new song of gladness."

Isn't that awesome! That's what David was talking about when he wrote, "He restoreth my soul."

To be a good leader,
you must first be led.

A Cloud by Day,
a Fire by Night!

I have a special shirt in my closet. No, I never wear it. In fact, the shirt is ruined, the front of it covered with black streaks and stains. But every now and then, I get it out and look at it. Those indelible stains remind me of how Paula and I received our ministry call for the city of Tampa. That now dingy garment symbolizes for us the assurance God gave that we were in the center of His perfect will.

That's why I treasure this "special" shirt and wouldn't give it up for anything.

One day I was looking through a Christian magazine when a simple classified advertisement caught my eye. A church in Tampa, Florida, was looking for a youth minister. That ad seemed to jump right off the page at me. At that moment, I began to realize that my destiny—God's plan for my life—was to unfold in Tampa. I called Paula on the phone and told her what had happened. She laughed, thinking I was playing a joke on her. Then she hung up.

To be honest, it seemed a little crazy to me as well. I had never been to Florida to minister in my life, not even during the time I was traveling extensively as an evangelist. We had no friends in Florida. I didn't even know anyone in Tampa. From what I'd heard, nothing ever happened in Tampa—it was a ministry graveyard. So to seriously consider moving to Florida on the strength of a four-line classified ad was totally illogical.

But I couldn't keep from thinking about it. The natural mind considers all the reasons not to do what God is saying to do. But we are not led by the mind. The Spirit of God is our Guide. If God says go, we must go. If God says do, we must do. If God says it will work, then it is right. All He asks of us is that we obey His Word.

I responded to the ad and found that the church was not in the denomination I'd been a part of—in fact, it was not even a full-gospel church. But the pastor was impressed with my background and experience and offered me the position. Now what was I going to do?

The church where Paula and I were ministering did not want us to leave. Knowing that we felt a burden and a calling to the people of the inner city, the pastor offered us a chance to develop such a ministry in our home city—even promising to provide a building downtown to get started.

It was so tempting to stay. We didn't want to leave our family and friends or our pastor, Dr. Lowery, whom we respect and love so much to this day. He had been a great help in our restoration process. Talk about getting out of our comfort zone! In the eyes of everyone we knew, going to work in a mainline denominational church as a youth pastor was a giant step backwards—a career killer. But I knew in my heart that God had spoken to me to go to Tampa, so Dr. Lowery sent us forth with his blessing.

We sold most of our things, settled our affairs, packed up our sentimental possessions in a U-Haul truck, and headed off to Florida. It was a long and terrible journey. We had just turned down a terrific ministry offer, said good-bye to our family and friends, left all that was familiar and comfortable, and headed for an uncertain future. Doubtful thoughts filled our minds. It was especially hard on Paula, who had not yet received a definite word from the Lord about Florida.

In the middle of that trip, she turned to me and said, "Randy, are you sure you have heard from God about this? I'll follow you to the ends of the earth as long as you are sure!"

There was a lump in my throat, and my eyes were stinging with unshed tears. All I could do was nod and blurt out, "I have heard from God!"

"Let's go to Florida," she said. In that moment, all doubt seemed to fade and a calm came into that truck. Though everything around seemed to point to disaster, we both felt at peace and confident that we were in God's will.

The new church and pastor in Florida welcomed us with open arms. And from the beginning, God gave us tremendous favor. The youth department in that congregation literally exploded in growth. People from all different races and backgrounds began showing up. There were even gang members who came to learn about the power of God. It was a tremendous experience. We soon began to realize that this was just the "first fruits," a foretaste of what was yet to come as God's plan unfolded.

HEARING FROM GOD

A few weeks after arriving in Florida, I went into a little chapel in the church to pray and consecrate myself to the Lord. I sensed that what was happening around me had taken me way out of my depth. I had a vivid awareness of what it must feel like to walk on the edge of a volcano—I could almost feel the ground rumbling and shaking beneath me as a totally unimaginable power was about to break through.

As I prayed, suddenly the glory of God fell upon me, and I simply floated and flowed in His presence. I lost all sense of time, being saturated completely in His overwhelming reality.

After a few hours, Paula wondered what had happened to me, and she came to find me. As she started down the hallway toward the chapel, she began to sense the presence of God permeating the atmosphere outside the chapel. As she stood there, she literally saw the Shekinah glory of the Lord like a cloud, and she smelled the sweet incense of His presence.

Hearing her approach outside, I crawled out of the chapel on my hands and knees. I was so overwhelmed by God's power that I could not stand. My hair was tousled, my clothes rumpled from lying on my face before the altar of God. My eyes were swollen from crying, and my face was streaked by the tears that had flowed like a fountain down my cheeks.

"What's happening, Randy?" she gasped. "What's going on?"

I told her, and I explained that God wanted to speak to us both. So we made our way back into the chapel to wait before the Lord.

After a time of praying together, a new sense of God's awesome presence rose up around us like a fog, and the fear of the Lord came upon us. I don't have the eloquence to describe what it was like. Paula and I held each other in our arms and wept until we had no more tears. Together, as one heart and one spirit, we consecrated our lives to God and His service, with no holding back. That day something broke, then surged and soared within us! We had come to where God had sent us . . . and He met us there.

Both of us sensed the word of the Lord ringing in our hearts. "I have called you to this place and to this city. Where you are now is a small piece of a larger puzzle. Although you cannot see all the pieces at this time, simply listen and be obedient to My voice, and I will guide you."

At some point during those hours, Paula's mascara began to mingle with her tears, running down her face and onto my shirt. Then, as now, those stains served as a visible reminder of that unspeakable experience when we were caught up together into the very presence of the Creator of heaven and earth and made aware that we, indeed, were in the center of His perfect will.

There were many lean and difficult days ahead. But never again have we ever doubted our call to take the city of Tampa for Jesus Christ. The path is not always smooth. Often the way is so dark before us that we cannot see even one step ahead. But like the children of Israel long ago wandering in the wilderness, we can see the cloud of God's glory as an assuring sign every day, and the fire of His presence is a beacon in the night. He is always with us.

Find the need and meet it.

The Day
of New Beginnings

When we went to Tampa as youth pastors, Paula and I gave ourselves to the task with all our hearts. We determined to be the best youth pastors who had ever had that job. It was a hard, demanding, tough job, with long hours and almost no time off. But we knew this was where God wanted us to be for the time being, and He helped us accomplish a great deal.

As the weeks and months went by, however, a sense of destiny grew within us. It became a driving force that could not find release in anything we were doing. From the day we had our remarkable spiritual encounter in the chapel, we began to cry out to God, "How long until You begin to work Your purpose in us? When will we begin what You've really called us to do?"

Many times individuals feel a special calling, or even receive a prophetic word about what they are to do. But God's plan is not always fulfilled right away. It's important not to get ahead of God, launching out prematurely, then getting discouraged and giving up.

I encourage people to be patient and faithful. If they will keep on doing what they can do, in God's time the doors of opportunity

Without Walls

will open. I often say that a man's ministry will make room for him!

By this time, both Paula and I were keenly aware that the reason God had sent us to Florida was to take the city of Tampa for Jesus. The magnitude of that task was staggering to us. How could two young people with no resources, no contacts, no visible means of support ever make an impact on an entire city? Surely we were totally inadequate to accomplish the task. But we could hardly wait to get started. We sensed that when God said it was time to begin, only then would we discover real meaning for our lives.

After several months, the pastor of the church where we were working decided to move on to another church. As he prepared to go, we felt a release to leave also and launch a whole new outreach to the city of Tampa. When we walked out of that place, we sensed we were stepping into our destiny.

But where were we supposed to go? How were we supposed to get started? We had no funds, no sponsors, and no income. All we knew to do was pray and expect God to lead us.

I WILL DO A NEW THING

> Behold, I will do a new thing; now it shall spring forth; shall ye not know it? I will even make a way in the wilderness, and rivers in the desert.
> —ISAIAH 43:19

A few days later, we felt led by the Holy Spirit to go visit Orlando Christian Center (now known as World Outreach Center), the very large, successful church pastored by Benny Hinn. During the service, Pastor Hinn called us out and began to prophesy to us. He said, "God has called you to take the city of Tampa. Do what is in your heart. You are sitting on a keg of dynamite with a short fuse. It's about to explode. Now is the time!" What a confirmation from God! We felt so encouraged.

Shortly afterward, Pastor Hinn sent a check for twenty-five hundred dollars for our ministry. We took that check and launched a new church, which we called South Tampa Christian Center. A man who owned an eleven-hundred-square-foot storefront space in a run-down, predominately vacant industrial area offered it to us free for a year. There was only one bathroom, one unfinished room that would be our nursery, an office that doubled as the children's church, a crude kitchen, and one larger room we used for worship.

Paula and I went to different local businesses, asking if they would donate materials to fix up the building. We received some lumber, paint, and wallpaper. We managed to get some folding chairs and a pulpit, some furniture for the nursery, and a makeshift desk and chair for the office.

With lots of hard work and the provision of God, we turned that storefront into a place of worship. It wasn't very big and definitely wasn't very fancy, but it was a start. That was the important thing.

Ours was a church of miracles from its very beginning. Its very existence was dependent upon supernatural provision. Hardly a day went by without some remarkable supernatural happening—including the necessary finances, materials, opportunities, and individuals being sent at just the right time.

During the first two years, there were never enough funds to provide a regular income for Paula and me. So in addition to trusting God for the resources to keep the church going, we also had to trust Him to provide for our personal needs.

We had nothing to start with, so we quickly learned the true meaning of living by faith. We gathered up some used, cast-off furniture—just the bare essentials. I'll never forget the "very used" mattress we had—the cover was ragged and "pee stained," and a broken spring poked through right in my back. I tried to keep it pushed down with a rag. We had a chair or two—no TV.

Money was so scarce that Paula and I saved and rolled pennies for gasoline—and fussed over who would face the embarrassment of going inside to pay.

At Christmas time, we couldn't afford to buy much as gifts—we didn't even have ten dollars for a Christmas tree. We were so surprised and thrilled when some friends showed up at our apartment with a little green tree and a few lights and decorations. It meant so much to four-year-old Bradley.

One day Paula called me and said, "Randy, there's no food in the house. What are we going to do?"

"There must be something—enough to get by today."

"There's absolutely nothing—not a can of tuna, not a box of Hamburger Helper—certainly not any hamburger meat. The cupboards are bare, and we're about to get hungry! I don't know what you want me to do."

"Pray, Paula, pray," I replied. "Don't tell me about it—tell Him. If He doesn't answer, we'll write a book about a first-time event and become millionaires. We'll call it *We Stepped Out on Faith and God Failed Us*. The Word says, '[I have not] seen the righteous forsaken, nor his seed begging bread'" (Ps. 37:25).

Paula was so exasperated with me that she hung up the phone. Then she remembered a teaching by Gloria Copeland about prophesying the answer to your need. So she went into the kitchen and started prophesying to the empty cabinets and refrigerator. She said, "Food is coming—good food...steaks, seafood, fresh vegetables, fruit, bread, and milk. Flour, sugar, and other staples are coming. Every shelf will be full of good food—no more junk, no make-do, no packaged macaroni and cheese. I believe that I receive it in Jesus' name."

Two hours later there was a knock at the door. People carried in boxes of food—good food, including fresh meat and seafood. "We thought you might need a few groceries," they said. The cabinet shelves, the refrigerator, and the freezer were filled with more food than we'd seen in months. And there was not a single box of macaroni and cheese!

Paula and I proved over and over the truth of God's promises, such as Luke 6:38: "Give, and it shall be given unto you; good measure, pressed down, and shaken together, and running over, shall men give into your bosom."

Shortly after we started the church, we volunteered to teach a seminar on children's ministry at a local Greek Orthodox church. At the end of the day, the church gave us a check for two hundred dollars. That may not sound like a lot, but after not having an income for a while, it seemed like a fortune to us.

That same night, we visited another church in Tampa. As the

minister was taking the offering, we sensed that God was speaking directly to us through his words. "Give all you have," he said, "and see what God will do."

When all you have in the world is two hundred dollars and you don't know when you will receive anything else, giving it all is a real faith challenge. But Paula was up to it. "God is telling me to give it all," she said to me quizzically.

"Then be obedient," I said.

She put our two-hundred-dollar windfall into the offering.

The very next morning, a woman walked into our little makeshift office and threw an envelope on my desk. "Take it!" she said. "God spoke to me to give this to you." After she left, I ripped open the envelope and found a check for ten thousand dollars! God had come through!

That wasn't the end, though. A few hours later, that same lady walked into my office again and threw another envelope on my desk. "I wasn't obedient to God the first time," she said. "Here's the rest of what He told me to give." I just sat there with a stunned look on my face as she walked out. Inside the second envelope was a check for five thousand dollars. In one day, God had given us a seventy-five-fold return on our two-hundred-dollar faith gift, which was all we had.

At that particular time, fifteen thousand dollars made the difference between surviving or sinking! And this is just one example of the way God provided for us. He has always been so faithful.

We must be fishers of men, not keepers of the aquarium.

Give Me Revival in This City, or Let Me Die!

In the early days of our church, I spent time every day praying for God to lead us to the people who needed us most—to make us a blessing and a light in the darkness. Early every morning, before most people were up, I would roll out of bed and go out walking through the streets of our neighborhood, praying and asking God for a great harvest.

What a sight I must have been—hair tousled, face unshaven, just the way I got out of bed! Dressed in jeans, T-shirt, and boots, I walked for miles, literally crying out to God, pleading for souls, praying in tongues. When, on occasion, I'd meet other early-morning walkers or joggers, they probably thought I was a crazy man. A couple of times people moved to the other side of the street to get away from me!

Every morning I asked the Father for my neighborhood, for the lost, for the broken and hurting, for those no one else cared about. I cried out for the Lord to use me to shake the city of Tampa by the power of God. Every morning I would claim the promise of John 15:16: "Ye have not chosen me, but I have chosen you, and ordained you, that ye should go and bring forth fruit, and that your fruit should remain: that whatsoever ye shall ask of the Father in my name, he may give it you."

I didn't want to build just another church made up of people who came from some other church. What sense did it make to be a keeper of the aquarium when Jesus had commanded us to be fishers of men? I wanted to cast my net into the deep—not to build a large church, but to make a difference in people's lives.

From the very beginning, I determined not to recruit other Christians. I wasn't after typical, churchgoing people. My sole intention was to win the lost, the sinners who needed Jesus. That's who I felt directed to go after. Paula and I resolved to "go out into the highways and hedges, and compel them to come in" (Luke 14:23).

So I walked the dingy streets of south Tampa and cried out to God, "Give me the derelicts, the undesirables of society. I want the misfits, the rejects, those who don't fit anywhere else. Give me the hurting, the broken, the prostitutes, those living out on the streets! Send me everyone that no one else wants. Give me revival in this city, or let me die!"

My wife says that often when I came in from praying on the streets, I looked like a madman. My clothes were windblown...my cheeks streaked with tears. I felt wrung out and spent, yet restless and driven. The vision was burning deep within me. I became completely convinced that God had promised me the needy, hurting people of my city as my harvest—that they would come to the saving knowledge of Jesus Christ.

I suddenly saw that my "fishing hole" contained 1.4 million souls—the entire population of the metropolitan Tampa area. I realized that when your motive really is just to make a difference in someone's life, God gives you a bunch of people in whose lives you can make a difference!

Our job is not to build a church but to impact the community.

If a Man Is Standing in the Rain, Give Him an Umbrella

After I'd been in Tampa a while, I was invited to preach one evening in a prominent local church. As an object lesson, I arranged for a young man from Without Walls to dress in ragged clothes and worn-out shoes and hang around the front doors of the host church. He looked exactly like the homeless people who wander the streets.

When the church people arrived, dressed in their fine clothes and religious dignity, they had to pass by the poor beggar to enter the church. There were about five hundred who attended the service that night—not one of them invited the stranger to come in. In fact, many of the arriving congregation were uncomfortable seeing him there; before long, he was asked to leave and stay off the church property. When he didn't go, someone called the police to have him removed. (I intervened with the pastor and the police to keep him from being hauled away to jail.)

That night I preached on evangelism and restoration. At the end of the message, I brought the young "beggar" in and told the people that I had put him at the door of the church, and that he had not been welcomed. "Why not?" I asked. "If a man is standing in the rain, don't criticize him for being wet—give him an umbrella!"

Then I asked, "Where would Jesus be if He came today? He would not ask, 'Where is the finest church?' He would say, 'Show me to the needy, the homeless mother, the prostitute!'"

Many repented in tears that night. However, several were indignant and angry that they had been confronted, and they left in a huff. A great many others were polite but cool as they passed me on their way out the door. I could not help feeling sad that many congregations of nice people like this one did not really have a vision to "rescue the perishing, care for the dying." They were not going out to passionately proclaim that "Jesus is merciful, Jesus will save."[1]

Sadly, American churches have too often multiplied by dividing. For too long, believers have been caught up in "playing church," swapping members with other congregations instead of really growing by adding new Christians to the body of Christ. Every church in America could be packed with people if pastors and church members went out into the community to love the despised and forgotten, to offer hope and help, and to minister the power of God to restore broken lives.

We must get out of our pews, out of our comfort zones, and go outside the walls of the church, out where the sinners are, out where the need is. Revival can happen...but not if we just sit around waiting. It depends on us. I promise that there is someone for you to reach if you really try to find him or her. It is time for the church—that's you and me—to realize that statistics and numbers are not really important, that choirs and decorations and programs are not our primary focus. What would happen if we concentrated on welcoming and winning the lost?

When I walked out of that fancy Tampa church that night, brokenhearted and disappointed that more had not responded positively, I felt stirred more than ever to go after the sin-sick and suffering that no one else seemed to want. And God gave them to us. Our church grew from five to seven hundred in the first year!

Randy White

OPERATION EXPLOSION

I'll never forget when God gave us the plan to reach the people on the streets. One Thursday evening, the Holy Spirit spoke to me to challenge our little congregation in the storefront church to reach out to the lost and the needy. That night, we raised an offering of twenty-four hundred dollars and used it to buy a big old truck.

You can imagine what kind of truck we could buy for only twenty-four hundred dollars. It was a 1974 model that was propane powered; whoever drove it had to shift from second to fifth gear because third and fourth didn't work. The steering linkage was very loose, which made keeping that truck in one lane quite a challenge. The brakes weren't the best, either. You needed a strong prayer life and a definite assurance of salvation to venture out behind the steering wheel of that vehicle. We called it "the Brontosaurus."

The truck had a huge twenty-four-foot box that we painted inside and out in bright colors. An artist who had just started attending the church volunteered to create artwork for the sides—colorful, cartoon-like characters to attract kids. We set up the inside of the big box van as a platform, or stage. After hours of work, we had a rolling sanctuary, a portable church to take into the public housing areas to conduct "sidewalk Sunday schools." We later called this outreach "Operation Explosion."

One of our first street meetings with the truck just about caused an explosion. A short time before we arrived, there had been a violent racial attack on an African American man in Tampa. He had been doused with gasoline and set on fire. There was a lot of racial tension around the community, and the inner city was boiling with unrest. One of the most turbulent areas was a public housing project called College Hill. Naturally, that's where we felt we should take our brightly decorated truck for a street meeting. Rather than being deterred by the circumstances, we felt God could use us to bring down racial barriers and lessen the tension. We wanted to demonstrate the love of God, realizing that people don't care how much you know until they know how much you care.

The day before, we went around the neighborhood to let everyone know we were coming and where we would be meeting.

Without Walls

We contacted the people in the entire area, door to door, face to face, eye to eye, putting promotional flyers printed on brightly colored paper in their hands. We enthusiastically explained what we would be doing and how exciting and enjoyable it would be.

Paula and I already knew from past experience that you must draw people in with personalized promotion—"baiting the hook." And you must use different bait for different fish. In this instance, we used candy and little toys to attract children and their parents. Lots of people promised to come.

When the truck rolled in the next day, a little group was waiting, and the kids came running. By the time we opened up the back of the truck and got everything set up, a pretty sizable crowd was gathering. And everybody on the ministry team was keenly aware of the presence and anointing of God.

Things started off well. There were colorful streamers, banners, balloons, and signs. We sang songs, played zany games, and found ways to involve the people of College Hill in the service. We even had plastic bags of water with goldfish to give to the kids.

Paula led the meeting that day. She felt strongly that God wanted us to show the people that our church loved all races and respected their different cultures and backgrounds. Using visual illustrations and simple object lessons, she talked about the unity of the body of Christ—that we are all one in His love. And the Spirit of God seemed to capture the hearts of the people.

As Paula was teaching, a wonderful African American brother stayed on the stage with her. Suddenly, a man at the edge of the crowd pulled out a gun and fired a shot into the air. There was no time for anyone to do anything to stop him. Two of our men instantly went to him, calming him down and talking to him. They even gave him a gift of some food we'd brought along—a loaf of bread and a pie. As they worked with him, the presence of the Lord was so powerful and evident in that place that the man was overwhelmed by it. He just melted, put his gun down, and began to weep. In the meantime, while all this was going on, Paula went right on with her lesson. God changed what could have been a very tragic situation into a breakthrough.

A short time later, a woman who was high on crack screamed,

brandishing a hypodermic needle. She was hysterical, screaming that she was an animal rights activist and that giving out the gold-fish was cruelty to animals. It turned out that she was just a broken, hurting woman. Her husband was in jail, and she had no one to help her with a houseful of unruly children. Someone cautiously went to the woman as Paula began to quietly speak the name of Jesus. Right away the distraught woman calmed down and handed over the needle. A little while later, she prayed with a ministry team member and gave her life to Christ.

The racial tension began to subside as the people saw the courage of our team and the obvious protective power of God. The love and anointing of God cut through the tension and anger and broke the yoke of strife and violence. Soon children and adults all around that rolling sanctuary were praying and seeking spiritual counsel. It was the first step toward literally hundreds of College Hill people accepting the Lord as their personal Savior.

The way this outreach ended up was a vivid confirmation of our belief that hunger and need are color-blind. If someone is drowning, he doesn't care what color the hand is that reaches out to save him.

As we packed up the truck to leave, the people milling around the area all repeated the same question, "When are you coming back? You will come again soon, won't you?"

Today the church has four Operation Explosion trucks that go into ten public housing areas, stopping in parks, fields, and parking lots around the government projects. Each truck has an evangelistic team of five to ten trained people who present a high-energy, fast-moving program, concentrating on loving and sharing with the people. Each truck goes out for services every day, several times on Saturday, and sometimes on Sunday afternoons. As many as three or four hundred kids gather at each site—as many as twenty-five hundred a week—to join in the fun and inspiration. They pay attention to the Bible stories and soak up the simple truth about Jesus and His gospel.

Public housing officials tell us that 12 percent of metropolitan Tampa's 1.4 million people live in the inner-city projects or other subsidized housing. Operation Explosion is impacting more than

60 percent of these residents—as many as one hundred thousand. The officials have asked us to expand our outreach into every public housing site.

The resident managers of the sites we visit say they can see dramatic changes taking place. The police confirm that there is less violence and fewer domestic problems, with a double-digit drop in the crime rate!

Today, after six years of consistent, faithful ministry, we are seeing the light of the gospel penetrating the darkness. It didn't happen overnight. And the battle is far from over. But it is working.

This is evangelism. This is Christian love in action. This is taking the church to the people. And if it works in Tampa, it will work anywhere.

---

1. "Rescue the Perishing" by Fanny J. Crosby. Public domain.

Pour into others what God has poured into you.

How Much More
Can God Call You?

Vicki has been part of Without Walls since the church was about six weeks old. Brilliant and unbelievably energetic, she immediately plugged in to what was going on. From the beginning, she never waited to be asked but rolled up her sleeves and got busy doing whatever needed to be done at the moment.

She helped pioneer the sidewalk Sunday school concept, which became our Operation Explosion; she is now our outreach pastor, supervising the section directors and the visitation teams that minister to hundreds of children each week in ten inner-city housing projects.

Vicki, along with her husband, Michael, helped launch several major "special event" outreaches, like the Christmas Extravaganza, the Back-to-School Bash, the World's Largest Easter Egg Hunt, and Kids Alive, a summer camp program for inner-city children. She is also vitally involved in the church's foster parent training program and other social care ministries.

Vicki knows how to work with the news media, how to publicize events, and how to interest and involve civic officials and political leaders in ministry outreach projects. She works closely with the creative and production people on our television program. In fact, she is knowledgeable about virtually every ministry and outreach, and she is constantly helping train and mentor leaders to assume responsibility.

Both Paula and I have learned to respect and appreciate Vicki's passion for hurting, needy people and her amazing capacity to handle details and get things done. We have poured into her from the depths of our heart and soul, and she has become an integral part of this ministry.

When she first came to us, however, she seemed an unlikely candidate to play a major role in an upstart, struggling, thirty-member church. Here was a beauty queen, winner of multiple pageants, a sorority girl, campus theater star, and a university cum laude graduate with career-position job offers from several major corporations. Why would she be drawn to a no-prestige, full-gospel church with makeshift facilities in a run-down industrial park?

Why did Vicki have such a vision to reach and help hurting, needy, underprivileged, unreached people, especially children? Because of where she came from and the work God did in her life.

Vicki was given up for adoption when she was three days old. In those days, seventeen-year-old unmarried mothers didn't keep their babies, especially when the "father" was a fifteen-year-old. Her adoptive parents wanted a family, but they hadn't been able to have children until shortly after they adopted her. Then her mother gave birth to a son, giving her two children within eleven months. Within another five years, another girl was born into the family.

Her adoptive father had serious personal problems—he was a perennial student, always away; even when he did come home, he was totally self-absorbed and withdrawn. He once went an entire year without speaking while he was working on a book project! Vicki's adoptive mom battled crippling rheumatoid arthritis; still she tried to fulfill the role of both father and mother, working hard to raise the three children and provide food, clothing, and an education for them. Vicki did not understand the stress and pressure her mother was under, and at times she felt unloved. As a result, communication was difficult for Vicki and her mom.

Vicki's brother and sister had fair skin, freckles, and red hair—completely different from her smooth complexion and long, dark hair. Insensitive people were always saying, "Oh, you're adopted, aren't you? Who are your real parents?" These tactless, insensitive comments caused Vicki to feel like an outsider, abandoned, rejected, and unloved, a powerless pawn in the unfeeling hands of fate.

Her adoptive grandmother felt a special closeness to Vicki. Extremely loving and supportive, she taught Vicki basic Christian truths and principles and took her to church. Although the bright, energetic, early-blooming girl became so troubled that she required psychological and emotional counseling all through her junior high and high school years, she was always aware of her grandmother's love and faith in God.

But by the ninth grade, Vicki became so distraught and discouraged that she consciously turned away from God, determining to make her own way in life by becoming an overachiever. She developed a "performance for acceptance" mentality, and over the next few years, she managed to attain virtually every goal she set for herself. But the honors and recognition she earned in academics, school social activities, and beauty pageants did not satisfy the deep yearning within her.

In high school, she began the first of three romantic relationships that turned out to be extremely abusive, destructive, and dangerous. Each lasted two years and reinforced the rejection and self-hate she felt. *This must all be my fault. No one can love me. I should never have been born. I'll never get better!* she thought to herself.

She was hammered by other tragedies as well. A man took several hostages in the shopping mall where she worked, and she was caught up in the six-hour siege. Eventually fourteen people died; Vicki witnessed some of them being shot, and she helped tend to bystanders who collapsed with chest pain because of the stress. It was a traumatic nightmare, leaving her with lingering scars.

Three days after graduation, three of her high school friends died in still another tragedy.

Desperate to make sense of her life and find her roots, Vicki managed to find and visit her birth parents. "That was the greatest experience of my life, except for when I was truly born again," she said. "My birth parents, who never married each other, were glad to see me. I got so many answers about who I was and why I acted and felt the way I did. I understood that my adoption was intended to be in my best interest."

But even this experience didn't "fix" everything. Vicki dived into college, still determined to overcome the darkness of her life through her own efforts. She excelled as a student and was dominant as a leader in student government, sorority, and social activities. She also had great success competing in beauty pageants, modeling for calendars, and appearing in commercials.

She graduated cum laude and was named the most outstanding business communications student out of a thirty-five-thousand-member student body. She was actively recruited by the human resource directors of several large companies and corporations.

But none of her accomplishments filled the spiritual void in her life. And she found no happiness.

Shortly before her graduation, Vicki had met the perfect man. Michael was strong but gentle, handsome and athletic, witty and fun loving, devoted and kind. In no time, they fell in love and began making plans to get married and climb the ladder of success together. For the first time in her life, Vicki felt that happiness might really be possible. Everything seemed to be working out, and the future looked bright.

WHEN DREAMS DIE

Then Michael was arrested, charged with a serious crime. To her horror and amazement, Vicki learned that he was deeply involved with dealing drugs. He worked in a health club, discreetly supplying drugs to a "respectable" clientele who were not comfortable shopping on the street.

Vicki had known that Michael traveled with a fast crowd, frequenting clubs and nightspots that were on the edge. In fact, with his muscle-man physique, he sometimes danced in clubs for fun before audiences of giddy, boisterous women out for a slightly scandalous good time, patterning his act after the notorious

"Chippendales." Although it was very profitable, Michael had always pursued it just for kicks.

But Michael had gotten caught up in a more sinister plot orchestrated by a friend he met at the health club. He was recruited to help his friend "get even" with a wealthy man by kidnapping an eleven-year-old child. The youngster was supposed to be invited out for the afternoon—the kidnap call made—then the boy returned home before he even knew he'd been captured.

The complicated scheme broke down, and Michael informed his friend he was out of it. But when the police found out about the attempted crime and questioned the others involved, they all blamed Michael. Since he was already under suspicion by the authorities for his drug-related activities, he was blamed for everything. The charges filed against him when he was arrested were so serious that his bail was set at one hundred thousand dollars. Vicki and Michael's friends couldn't afford to arrange his bail.

The whole incident was too much for her to handle. It totally knocked her off her feet. She sat in her grandmother's house, not knowing what to do or how to pick up the pieces of her shattered life. For years she had tried to be totally self-confident and self-reliant, the one who could fix any problem on her own. Now she felt helpless, depressed, and distraught—at the absolute end of herself.

She turned on the television and began watching *The 700 Club*. Sheila Walsh came on and said, "Are you going through terrible trouble and don't know how you are going to face the day? Have you exhausted all your resources? If you're running from the Lord, it is now time to come back to Him."

Everything Sheila said described Vicki's situation and caused her to break completely. Then Sheila said, "I want you to rededicate your life to God. It's time to come home." So Vicki prayed with her. She'd tried doing things her way, but she couldn't do it any more. As she sat crying out to God, Sheila began to sing "Come Home!"—a song she'd never heard before. As Vicki said, "How much more can God call you?"

While waiting through the long months before Michael's trial, Vicki began attending different churches. She desperately wanted to be in the will of God and have Him take control of her life. She was searching for a place to find spiritual reality and be sure she was part of God's plan and purpose. But none of the churches she visited seemed right for her. She'd always moved at a fast pace, and every place she tried was a letdown, lethargic and inactive.

Then someone gave her tickets to a banquet being held by a new church, then called South Tampa Christian Center. Desperate for fellowship, she decided to attend. When she walked into the entryway, she saw display panels promoting the vision and outreach of the church. This small but ambitious new congregation either already had—or was planning—a prison ministry, homosexual outreach, AIDS patients ministry, singles ministry, divorce counseling, children's ministry, youth ministry, and an inner-city outreach.

She shook her head in amazement. Here were some people who practiced practical Christianity, a make-a-difference, do-some-good kind of faith. She'd never heard of such a church. This was exactly what she was looking for. She hurried into the banquet to find out how she could get involved and be part of what God was doing.

When Vicki got so excited and wanted to get involved, we weren't sure how long her enthusiasm would last. Was she just a "do-gooder" who would start strong but fade fast?

Doing the work of the ministry is not nearly as glamorous and flashy as many folks think. Mostly it's hard, tough, grueling, grinding work, with little appreciation or recognition. Many people are overwhelmed by the sights, sounds, smells, and heartbreaks of dealing with the problems and needs of suffering people.

Both my father and Pastor T. L. Lowery had taught Paula and me to let people prove themselves by performance and faithfulness rather than promises and good intentions. They taught us to find out if people were really working for the Lord . . . or for prestige and profit.

In my early association with Dr. Lowery, I was a gung-ho, "wannabe" preacher with a pretty optimistic opinion of my value and potential. I was so excited when the pastor asked if I could help him with a project on Sunday. Envisioning some task that might bring me attention and a chance to show what I could really do, I was quick to volunteer.

Randy White

"After the service, I want you to go through the wastebaskets in the nursery and childcare areas and take out all the dirty diapers. Put them out back in the garbage can. The cleaning service charges extra if they have to handle those diapers."

What a letdown. Instead of basking in the spotlight, I went all alone to perform what I felt was a disgusting, degrading task. And Dr. Lowery managed to come up with several more such pride-deflating jobs along the way. His philosophy was, "Before you preach in my pulpit, be willing to clean my bathrooms!"

The apostle Paul admonished, "And we beseech you, brethren, to know them which labour among you..." (1 Thess. 5:12). The best way to know someone, I've found, is to invite him or her to come work beside me—to roll up his sleeves, get dirty, and get the job done. This shows where his heart is and what he's made of.

That's what Paula and I did with Vicki. When this bright, brilliant, beautiful girl—who could have had her choice of top-paying jobs—kept coming around asking how she could help, we gave her some tough, mundane, thankless chores. She did them and asked for more. Then she became a volunteer staff member—she worked a full schedule of hours for ten months without pay, achieving excellence every day. Then we started paying her—not much, but all we could afford. With the many hours she put in, some weeks her pay would have been less than a dollar an hour.

God has blessed Vicki for her devotion and sacrifice, providing for and prospering her and her family in many ways.

To this day, I seldom pay much attention to the resumés people send in or to the calls from those who want to know if we are hiring. There is little room for hirelings in the church without walls. When more workers and leaders are needed, I believe the answer is "in the house." We maintain an intensive, thorough training program for new converts and members who want to learn how to do God's work. As much as possible we hire and promote from within.

Our goal is to be
the perfect church
for people who are
not perfect.

The
Vegetable-Soup
Church

There are plenty of hurting people. Homeless. Hungry. Sick. Disturbed. Drifters and luckless types. Single parents struggling to barely get by. Families that can't get along. Kids who have fallen through the cracks. Drug users and drunks. Ex-cons who can't get a new start in life. Prostitutes who want to break free of pimps.

On the other hand, there are lots of "regular" people—respectable Christian folks with jobs and middle-class homes, two cars, and three kids. They are looking for something—anything—to give their lives meaning and purpose, some kind of significance. They are on a spiritual search, looking for a church home where they can not only be nurtured, but where they can put their talents to work and help change the communities they live in.

God put it in my heart to bring the two groups together. Paula and I started Without Walls International Church in 1991 (then South Tampa Christian Center) in an eleven-hundred-square-foot space in a strip mall off Manhattan Avenue. There were five people at the first service, including us.

Without Walls

We put signs along the road and flyers on front doors and car windshields, inviting the unchurched and unconverted to visit "the perfect church for people who are not." From the beginning, we went after the people no other church wanted—the outcasts, the ostracized, the down-and-outs, the people without "Sunday" clothes who didn't smell so good...and might not even know how to act during a service.

At first they stayed away in droves. Then the curiosity seekers started slipping in to look around and see what kind of strange religious people these were who welcomed everybody with open arms, without reservation.

Many of those who came just to check us out ended up staying and getting involved. And our attendance rapidly ballooned from a handful to a houseful. We found ourselves reaching a wide variety of people, from felons just out of prison to Tampa Bay Buccaneers players to doctors to former motorcycle gang leaders. There were also lots of ordinary people from ordinary neighborhoods and ordinary churches who were looking for something extraordinary. And they found it. At Without Walls, people of all backgrounds and cultures, rich and poor, African Americans, Whites, and Hispanics worship—and work—side by side. We really could be described as "the vegetable-soup church"—a little bit of this, a little bit of that. It was—and is—a most unconventional atmosphere.

WHAT DO YOU DO WITH A CRACK BABY?

When you start ministering to the "undesirables" of society, you begin encountering some unforeseen situations right away. The children of the inner city became one of our first outreach targets, and we soon began attracting substantial numbers of mothers with babies and toddlers.

In most churches, the nursery is a baby-sitting club that cares for young children while their parents attend service. It quickly became obvious that at our church, which was reaching out to the lost in the world, the nursery was going to be different.

Paula soon discovered that she couldn't just round up volunteers to watch the children in our nursery. We had crack babies being dropped off—sickly, irritable, tormented infants who screamed nonstop at the top of their lungs. There were babies who had not been held or cuddled for months—maybe never.

We had babies who were children of AIDS patients. We had a baby with gonorrhea who had been infected from its mother during birth. There was nothing "routine" about caring for these children. These infants had to be handled skillfully; these babies' diapers had to be changed with great care.

What do you do with a crack baby? What do you do with infants who are HIV positive? Do they present special health risks? How do you handle babies infected with gonorrhea? Suddenly we realized that the workers in our nursery needed special training. We had to have nurses come in and teach our attendants how to deal with special needs and conditions. They had to use gloves, antiseptic wipes, and special ointments. Our nursery workers had to be trained to meet the physical and hygienic demands, and they had to learn how to minister to these little ones spiritually, lovingly, in prayer.

In our nursery, fretful, irritable, suffering babies from God-only-knows-what conditions begin to respond to the loving touches, the compassionate words and songs, the healing prayers of faith. Many of them start relaxing and being more at peace; they start eating better and sleeping better.

Working in our church nursery has to be a special calling—much more than just volunteering a couple of hours every week. Our nursery is front-line spiritual warfare, a deliverance room in the Spirit realm. Only people who are prepared and prayed up can function successfully there, where a Spirit-filled ministry is in operation just as much as in the main services.

MAKING DISCIPLES

As Without Walls experienced supernatural growth, we soon recognized that a major problem was getting people trained in how to live a Christian life. The people we were winning were not believers coming from other churches. For the first two years, 80 percent of those who came to us were first-generation new converts. They had never been discipled. They were not from solid, stable backgrounds, but from the extremes of sin, problems, and crisis. Most had come from dysfunctional homes that hadn't taught them even the basic social skills and moral values, much less any traditional religious practices and jargon. They were brand-new babies, bringing with them all the problems associated with the newly saved.

God said, "It is time to disciple those you have been given. I am not going to give you any more until you do."

As a result, we began to raise up a number of specialized ministries to meet the needs of the people. They needed counselors to help them with deep personal problems. Some still needed deliverance from oppression, addictions, and bondage. Some needed marriage guidance, help with financial management, employment direction, family relations therapy, and much more.

Where do you get the staff to provide so many urgently needed services? Yes, some functions require a full-time paid professional. Today Without Walls has some eighty ministers and workers on staff. But we operate more than two hundred ministry outreaches to the congregation and the community. Some of these individual services and ministries each require dozens of workers. So where do we get them?

Most are volunteers, unpaid lay ministers. And we have an aggressive, ongoing training program to grow our own workers.

Right from the beginning, we established the Master Pastor Internship Program (MPIP). This is a one-year intensive training course designed to help people find their calling, discover their destiny, follow their vision, and learn how to lead. Knowing we had potential leaders sitting in our congregation, we set out to qualify and train them for service.

The first year, we had one hundred twenty students who attended five hours of teaching and training workshops weekly, receiving both basic theory of ministry as well as practical, hands-on training and experience. We have acquired most of our present pastors and staff workers, as well as a high percentage of our volunteer staff members, from within the congregation through MPIP training.

One MPIP graduate named Megan wanted to be an extension

of the church without walls and make a difference in other people's lives. She started a group called Corporate Evangelism Outreach, or CEO. Megan helped set up and direct weekly Bible studies for professional people. Dozens meet together at various locations to study, pray, and provide encouragement and accountability to each other. Not all of them attend our church, but that is the reason for being a church without walls. Our goal is to help people find Jesus and have their needs met.

Megan is now a paid staff member at the church, serving as our receptionist. Handling our phone system and keeping track of the comings and goings of our ministry team is an enormous challenge. She felt God was directing her to leave her corporate position and take a cut in pay to provide this ministry service.

MPIP has been a unique and wonderful success story. We decided to set up the school as an accredited training center so the students attending could build up credits that could transfer to a college of their choice. Normally this process takes four to five years. But God gave us favor with the official body for the State of Florida that oversees this operation. After we submitted our course prospectus and graduated our first class, our MPIP course received full accreditation.

Since then we've been able to help churches in many areas start similar programs. Each year many hundreds of new ministers are being trained and sent into the fields that are white unto harvest.

I didn't get my youth
minister out of
seminary—I got him
out of prison!

Don't Look Back!

Michael isn't the typical church youth pastor. I didn't hire him from another church or out of seminary. But his impressive "iron pumping," bodybuilding, and strongman feats, his experience as a drug abuser and dealer, and his time behind prison walls gave him unique qualifications to minister to the young people Without Walls is trying to reach. These are kids who know firsthand about drugs and gangs, about crime and cops and the court system.

Michael was totally streetwise. Although up to his eyebrows in the drug culture, he was so charming and smooth that his fianceé, Vicki, had absolutely no idea. Not Michael! He worked out in the gym every day and ate healthy—he wouldn't even put a cookie in his mouth. How could he be a big-time user of marijuana, cocaine, Ecstacy, and "acid," or LSD?

To Vicki, he was the perfect sweetheart—funny, loving, gentle, and kind. They planned to get married after she graduated from college and climb the ladder of success together.

Despite his smooth, unruffled exterior, Michael's life had never been tranquil. His birth father had never been around, and his mother was an alcoholic and into drugs. His grandmother was the stable person in the family, and Michael lived with her off and on throughout his childhood when things were too tough at home.

In high school, when Michael was just achieving success as a varsity football player with a promising future, his mom and stepfather withdrew him from school one day and told him he was moving from California to Florida. His grandmother was dying of ovarian cancer, and he was needed to help care for her. She died nine months later.

Immediately, his parents announced they were getting a divorce. Michael's stepfather and half-brother were to live together, and Michael was to stay with his mom. He had no vote in the matter and was crushed at being separated from his brother.

Michael's mother spent all her money—and the money Michael's grandmother had left for him—on her drug and alcohol habits. So Michael moved out on his own, dropping out of high school to work and support himself. All his dreams and aspirations of a football career crashed. His whole life was in shambles…and he was only seventeen.

Michael found a job working in a health club. There he met a major drug dealer who cunningly drew Michael into selling drugs—paying him more in a three-day period than he could earn in several months of forty-hour weeks.

Michael soon discovered that his health club position was a perfect cover for drug dealing, and he got more and more involved.

When he found out the police were watching his activities, waiting for him to slip up, Michael got scared and quit for a while. A friend helped him find a new way to make money—as a male dancer in nightclubs. With his powerful physique, boyish good looks, and Chippendale style, he was very popular with the patrons. He was interviewed by agents for possible modeling assignments and for an audition to act on a TV soap opera. This became his new goal.

During this time, he met the charming Vicki and fell head over heels in love. They conducted much of their courtship via long distance while she was completing her college degree. But they shared big plans for success and planned to get married after she graduated. For many months their lives seemed to be going well.

Then Michael got back on drugs, and within weeks he was on a downward spiral, out of control. He felt defeated and depressed; he even began to have suicidal thoughts. At nineteen, he felt his life was over.

Through a bizarre series of events, while trying to help a friend, he got involved in a fake kidnapping scam involving an underage boy. When the police broke up the clumsy crime, the other people involved blamed everything on Michael. Michael was arrested and his bail was set at one hundred thousand dollars. There was no way Vicki or his friends could raise that kind of money.

God was arranging a divine appointment for Michael...in jail.

Several days later, an elderly African American man who was the jail chaplain began to talk to Michael about God and how the Lord Jesus Christ could help him turn his life around. In a classic jailhouse religion story, this chaplain prayed with him to be "born again"—and Michael found the Lord.

The next morning, he called Vicki to tell her what had happened to him. To his astonishment, he learned that she had responded to a Christian telecast the night before and had rededicated her life to Christ. And she had vowed to break off her relationship with Michael unless the Lord saved him that same night!

Michael's trial was delayed for several months; during this time Vicki began attending various churches in Tampa. That's when she got involved with Paula and me at what was to become Without Walls International Church.

By the time Michael was released after spending a total of eighteen months in jail and prison, Vicki had become a regular at the church, totally involved in ministering to children—something she had always said she'd never do. He quickly fit into the outreach ministries of the church, volunteering to do whatever needed to be done, asking nothing but an opportunity to serve.

At first that amounted to cleaning up the building, scrubbing the toilets, being a "go-fer," doing the jobs no one else wanted to do. He was always willing and faithful. At the same time, Michael was learning—reading his Bible voraciously, taking Bible study classes, observing and asking questions, participating in various group outreaches, preparing himself for ministry. He was a natural leader, gifted and resourceful.

Without Walls

After a time of proving himself, Michael was given a place of service at the church. Like Vicki, he worked as a volunteer for many months before becoming a paid staff member. Michael had an uncanny rapport with young people, being able to make them laugh, to "speak their language," and to relate to their interests and problems. "Knowing where I'd come from, kids believed me when I told them I understood what they were going through," he said. "And they'd pay attention when I said God could help them get through any situation they faced."

In addition to leading the youth activities at the church, Michael helped organize a group of "strongmen" to perform in schools and youth centers. Using feats of strength, bending steel bands and breaking bricks with their bare hands, the Conquering Force captures the attention of its young audience, then delivers a potent anti-crime, anti-drug presentation. The group members talk about coping with peer pressure, avoiding violent situations, achieving personal potential, and developing self-respect. Kids get the message and respond positively to the veiled witness, with the enthusiastic approval and endorsement of school leaders and city officials.

Michael also directs "Club X," a church-sponsored weekend hangout for teens. The club provides a drug-free, alcohol-free environment filled with top-line lighting and contemporary music, as well as a food court, videos, games, and a youth staff prepared and ready to just talk and listen. Club X may not be a conventional, orthodox ministry outreach, but every young person who comes is exposed to the gospel.

When Michael and Vicki got married, they had a ready-made family. Vicki had been caring for two African American boys whose mother had "given" them to her to raise. Because the mother often disappeared for long periods of time, they applied to be foster parents. Although Michael frequently refers to his criminal record and provided Florida's Department of Health and Rehabilitative Services (HRS) his fingerprints and social security number, the agency later revoked their foster care license, saying he misled them by signing a good moral conduct affidavit. They took the children out of the home.

Three busloads—some two hundred fifty members—of the church congregation showed up outside the HRS office to protest the action and to support Michael and Vicki. They also sent more than two hundred letters on their behalf. The stand they took helped influence the situation. Eventually, after an eight-month ordeal, the children were returned to their home.

Both Michael and Vicki are passionate promoters of Christian couples becoming foster parents or adopting homeless kids. "If Christians don't take these kids, the devil's people will," said Michael.

"That's right," exclaimed Vicki. "Social service agencies are giving kids to those who ask for them because the need for parents and care-givers is so great. There are eight thousand children in our state who need adoption—twelve hundred in foster care in our county alone. So kids are being placed with very dysfunctional couples. The church has got to mobilize its forces to get involved in practicing what it preaches."

In addition to his work as youth pastor, head of Club X, and directing the Conquering Force outreach to public schools, Michael spends a great deal of time and effort helping establish similar ministries in other churches around the world.

He has established and trained fifteen "strongman" ministry teams in Washington, Florida, Hawaii, and other areas that are already getting tremendous results in their respective areas. One team, the Men of War in Hawaii, has eighty Samoan athletes involved, and it is becoming internationally recognized for the effectiveness of its dramatic presentation. The team members have presented their Christian testimony before many foreign visitors and have been invited to perform for the president of the United States.

Michael has also helped other churches set up Christian teen outreaches patterned after Club X. In Johannesburg, South Africa, Christian Family Church saw its youth group multiply from fourteen to more than a thousand in just a few weeks when the church opened its Club J (for Jesus). In fact, one-third of the congregation is now made up of youth, and the teen cell groups are growing so fast that it is difficult to train leaders quickly enough to keep up.

The Without Walls concept of ministry really works. And as Michael is helping to prove, it works in Tampa, in Washington, in Hawaii, in South Africa—anywhere people dare to do whatever it takes to reach the lost and meet the need.

You only need
God to do what
only God can do.

Nothing Left but Ashes

David, king of Israel, God's chosen servant, was in trouble again. He had sinned by disobeying God and ordering a census of Israel, from Beersheba to Dan. When Israel's enemies rose up against him, David said, "All right, we're getting ready to go to battle—how many numbers do we have? How many soldiers can we put on the battlefield?"

Trouble is sure to come when a man says, "How much do I have? How large are my resources?"

There is a certain sense of security in knowing that you have enough. But if you trust in enough, God will see that you never quite have it. Your sufficiency must be in Jehovah God alone.

God does His best work when you don't have enough. The greatest miracles He ever performs happen when you don't have enough. God is attracted to people who don't have enough.

Remember this—you don't need God to do what man can do. If man can work it out, God will let him. If man can figure out an answer, God says, "Go ahead." It's only when man has reached the end of his wisdom and his hoarded resources that God steps in.

You Only Need God to Do What Only God Can Do!

When David sinned through his disobedience, there were consequences to pay. In this case, God gave David three choices. He said, "Choose the punishment for your sin. You can endure three years of famine, or three months under the enemy's sword, or three days under My judgment. Take your pick."

David said, "That's a no-brainer. I know that I messed up. I know there is a price to be paid. But I'll take my chances in casting myself upon God's mercy rather than to let myself fall into the hands of men."

Don't think David got off easy. His sin was worshiping numbers, of trusting in the amassed forces of Israel's fighting men. The punishment of God was the destruction of some of those numbers—seventy thousand of them. The plague struck people down the length and breadth of the country. The very thing David had been tempted to trust was taken away.

David grieved for his people and cried out to God to put the punishment on him alone, not on them. Then he praised and worshiped the Lord. And God stayed the hand of the death angel.

I can imagine the angels in heaven saying, "God, what are You going to do with David? He messed up and deserves Your wrath. Are You going to pour out Your judgment on him as he deserves?"

And God says, "I know that he deserves wrath and judgment, but he's worshiping Me. He keeps writing Me love songs. He keeps taking Me out dancing every night. He keeps praising My name. What can I do with a man like that? I've got to show him My mercy. I've got to restore him again. I've got to give back to him the joy of My salvation one more time!"

Take a lesson from David. When you mess up and fall short, get on your knees and start worshiping God. I call it crazy praise! When you know you don't even have a right to worship God, worship Him all the more. When you feel isolated and away from God, just keep saying, "I know You're still on the throne, God. You've got everything under control."

Are you facing a dilemma? Maybe your finances don't add up. Or your marriage partner says that love has died. Or everything you've worked for is falling apart. Start praising God. Give Him crazy praise, radical praise. Sing to God. Dance before Him. Raise up your hands and your heart before him. It doesn't make sense, of course. But God will hear you. He will see you. And He will show you grace and mercy.

God told David, "Go to the threshing floor and build Me an altar. You don't have to stay in your sin against Me."

What is a threshing floor? It was a place where the harvesters would pound the wheat to separate the grain from the chaff. Then they'd throw it into the air and let the wind blow the debris and waste away, and the kernels of grain would fall to the floor to be taken into the storehouse.

All of us must have our turn on the threshing floor. God allows the trials, tests, and tribulations to pound us and shake us loose from the debris in our lives. The threshing floor is not for sissies. It can be a bruising experience. But after a time, the blows and grinding of the threshing floor do their work, separating us from the relationships that ruin our lives and from the impurities that ruin our values. God separates us from the chaff, and the wind of the Holy Spirit comes to blow away the debris. And the separated kernels of our lives fall down to be gathered into God's keeping, to be saved and used by Him.

So David went to the threshing floor, which belonged to a man named Ornan the Jebusite. He told him what God had said, that he was to build an altar there and make a sacrifice to the Lord. Ornan said, "Take what you need. Take the threshing floor. I'll provide all you need to build the altar and the wood for the fire. I'll even round up some oxen for the sacrifice. It's all yours for the taking. I'll give it to you."

David said, "Thanks, but I'll pay you the full value for these things. I can't take your possessions to give to the Lord. I cannot give God something that cost me nothing!" And he bought it all for the full price—six hundred shekels of gold.

So David built an altar, made a fire, offered burnt offerings and peace offerings, and called upon the Lord. The Bible says God answered him from heaven by fire upon the altar. And when it was over, there was nothing left but ashes.

Without Walls

Are you ready to sacrifice everything to God...and give it all to Him? You may be broken and hurting. Sin may have laid you low. You've been on the threshing floor and now you're going through the fire. But God's about to bring you out, purged of all the impurities and weaknesses. Everything that can be burned will be, and there'll be nothing left but ashes. But what seems to be the end is only a new beginning.

When David walked off the threshing floor of Ornan the Jebusite, there was nothing left but ashes and brokenness. But the Bible says that God allowed Solomon to build a great temple, a house for the Lord, on top of the ashes of David, his father. Solomon and his artisans and craftsmen took a great fortune in cedar and gold and precious stones, the most fabulous riches and the finest building materials. For seven years, they labored to build the most splendid structure that has ever been erected on this earth. But underneath it all—beneath the carved beams, woven tapestries, and gold sheathing—was a field of ashes, all that was left of David's sacrifice.

God has been so good to Paula and me. Starting with nothing and coming back from personal failure, we have been used of God to establish a church that is making a difference in our community and helping prepare workers for the harvest across the nation.

Beneath it all—the accolades of the mayor and civic leaders, the acquisition of buildings and property, the focused attention of television exposure, the cover story in ministry publications, and other national publicity—is brokenness and ashes!

When God wants to do something great, He looks for ashes. He looks for brokenness. God will take the ashes of your life and give you great victories. On the burned-out ruins of your broken dreams, He will raise up something beautiful.

There are two kinds of people—boat-sitters and water-walkers.

Christmas Extravaganza

During the second year of our church, we had a Christmas party for about three hundred fifty kids from several inner-city sites. We had decorations, music, and lots of food and refreshments. We also presented each child with stockings, candy, and a small toy. That was all we could afford, but the children were genuinely grateful as they went home.

Michael and Vicki, our dynamic duo, invited some of the older kids over to their home for the evening after the party. As youth pastor and outreach pastor, they just wanted to bless the kids with a little special attention, and they all just sat around the house talking and laughing for hours.

After midnight the phone rang, and Vicki answered it. It was a friend she had not seen or spoken to in years calling to wish her a merry Christmas. Then the person said, "I heard you are in the ministry now. I don't know if you're interested or not, but I have two semitrailer trucks full of brand-new toys. I've got to get rid of them before Christmas. Would you like to take them off my hands?"

Without Walls

Responding in her usual energy and enthusiasm, Vicki exclaimed, "Yes, we'll take them. We know lots of kids who need toys!" And she made arrangements to meet the trucks and unload the precious cargo.

It was now nearly one o'clock on the morning of Christmas Eve. Most people were sleeping, resting up for a time of holiday enjoyment with family and friends. But not Michael and Vicki. By daylight they had worked out a plan for a once-in-a-lifetime Christmas Extravaganza for needy parents and children.

By nine o'clock, Michael was talking to the manager of the nearby Roberd's furniture warehouse, asking to borrow their largest delivery van. When he explained the situation, the man amazingly said yes. In the meantime, Vicki was on the phone, calling church members, asking them to cancel their personal plans and come help with the toys.

While Michael and several guys started hauling the toys from the semitrucks to the church, Vicki's volunteers were clearing a place inside the building that housed the church. They sorted the toys, removing those that were violent or unsuitable. But there were still fifteen thousand brand-new, expensive toys left. There were footballs, basketballs, dollhouses, remote-control cars, toy shopping carts, huge dolls, electronic games—all the popular "in" toys for that year. They set up big folding tables and put the toys on and under the tables, arranged by age group and type.

Vicki had mobilized other volunteers to go to the public housing projects and make it known that there would be free toys available at the church that night. She also had asked a local television station to help publicize the event. "Oh, thank God for what you're doing," said the manager. "There is so much need out there. We'll be glad to help publicize this." The station kept running the announcement for people to come to the church that evening at seven o'clock if they couldn't afford to buy toys for their children.

That night it was cold and raining, but there was a massive line of people waiting. A church worker would take one family at a time through the toy wonderland, helping them pick out three toys for each child. Then the worker would minister Jesus to them, praying with each parent or family. They helped carry the toys out, walking with the family out to their car or cab. The workers waited on and served the people as if they were the most important folks in the city.

There were lots of tears that night. Literally hundreds of poor parents said, "You don't know what this means to us! We only had a few dollars to live on—there was no money to buy toys for our kids." Some people came in drunk, saying, "We couldn't stand facing our children without any presents to give them." There were even welfare workers who came by to thank us because they had run out of toys to give to needy families.

The line was long, and it moved slowly. But God provided help. Members of the church whom we'd been unable to contact saw the TV news report of what we were doing and rushed down to the church to help us.

About eleven o'clock that night, we began to run out of toys, but there were still about fifty families waiting. Vicki couldn't stand the thought of turning them away. So she rounded up a team to go out and bring back more toys.

They thought she was a little bit crazy. "Vicki, where are we going to find toys this late on Christmas Eve? How are we supposed to pay for them?"

"Get going!" she ordered. "God will lead you to some place that will help." So off they went.

After finding most stores closed and dark, they eventually found one Phar-Mor store still open. They rushed in and asked the manager for toys, explaining what was going on and how there were still fifty families who didn't have gifts for their children. As it turned out, he had been watching the whole story on TV. He said, "I'm going to get into big trouble, but grab some carts."

The next fifteen minutes were bedlam as our workers ran up and down aisles, filling up the shopping carts with toys. They loaded them into cars and rushed back to the church just in time.

Every child who came to our church that night left with three nice, expensive toys. Single mothers who had no one to turn to for help cried openly as they picked out gifts for their kids. Big, burly guys who were out of work stood by the toy tables, rubbing their eyes, shoulders heaving with silent sobs.

Overwhelmed with emotion and gratitude, many parents just kept saying, "Oh, thank you, thank you. God bless you." Several reported that they had prayed, "God, if You're really real, please help our children get at least one present!"

As our workers prayed with them, some asked the Lord into their hearts and received the most precious gift of all!

The TV crew that had been covering the toy giveaway continued the story the next day. They went to the homes of some of the families, interviewed the parents, and showed the kids happily playing with the toys they had received. The TV station reported that what they called the "Secret Santa" program had reached at least a thousand families.

People still stop me on the street and say, "You probably don't remember me, but your church gave toys to my children at Christmas when we had nothing. Thank you. It meant so much, and we'll never forget what you did."

Of course, the Christmas Extravaganza has become an annual event. To this day, it is one of our most popular and rewarding ministries.

People don't care how much you know—until they know how much you care.

Does God Love Nobodies?

When we met Suzanne, she was married to the government. Her only income was from welfare, food stamps, and aid for dependent children checks. She had never been away from her five children or out of Central Park, the inner-city public housing project where she lived.

You had to be "somebody" to get out and go places and do things. And she was a "nobody"—no resources, no talents, no skills, and no hope. Once she had dreamed about getting out of the ghetto and making a new life for herself and her kids, but she didn't know where to start or what to do. So the dream slowly died, and Suzanne just gave up.

Day after day, she sat in the squalor of her unkempt tenement, ignoring the constant squabbling of her undisciplined brood of restless offspring. Without even enough self-esteem to make friends with her neighbors, she stayed mostly to herself. Her only visitors were depression and despair.

Then one day a big pink truck rolled into Central Park and a bunch of energetic young people jumped out. Pretty soon music was playing and the side of the truck opened up to reveal a platform. The workers brought out banners and balloons, and a clown and other characters began bantering with the gathering crowd of neighborhood children and their parents.

"What's that?" asked Darla, Suzanne's oldest child. "Let's go see," cried Marcus and Mario. "Take Keith with you," said Suzanne as her daughter Brianna started out the door.

In a couple of hours they were back, chattering in excitement. There had been games and contests, singing and dancing, laughter and food! Everybody got the chance to join in. They had talked about God. Best of all, they were coming back next week!

Sure enough, the Operation Explosion team did return week after week. Who was doing this? And why? One day Suzanne decided to go along just to see these people who were so kind to her children. She really liked them—their fun-loving antics even made her smile. And they talked about God as if He were a real person.

Before long, someone from the outreach team came to Suzanne's front door for a short visit. She hardly knew how to act or what to say. But they were so warm and friendly they made her feel at ease. They wanted permission to pick up her kids on a bus the next Sunday and take them to church.

Suzanne was a little reluctant. Her kids had never been anywhere, and they didn't know how to act around other people. "Please, Mama, say yes," they pleaded. "We want to go." So finally she agreed.

When the bus picked up the children on Sunday, Suzanne halfway expected them back early. *Those kids don't behave, and the church folks are not going to put up with that,* she thought. *They'll dump them back here and not have anything else to do with them.*

And the kids were a handful! But the more they acted up, the more our children's workers loved them. More than anything else, underprivileged kids need love and attention. They're starving for it.

After sending her kids off to church every Sunday for a month or so, Suzanne decided to go along. It was a big adventure for her, venturing out of the project, being around other people, having someone else look after the kids. She loved the music and the singing in the church service. She felt something strange when the people prayed. And to her surprise, she could understand what the preacher was talking about.

So she went back again. The teaching and encouragement of Pastor Paula was especially meaningful to Suzanne. Could it really be true that God knew who she was and loved her? Was that why all these people were treating her as if she was worth something? They knew where she had come from—they picked her up. Why were they doing this?

Slowly, week after week, Suzanne began to learn about God's love and His plan for her life. She was suspicious and skeptical at first. A few times she dropped out and stayed home. But the kids were totally captivated and loved going to church. So Suzanne kept coming back, too.

After several months, some of the ladies at Without Walls invited her to a women's retreat. They gave her a scholarship, provided a few toiletries, and arranged for someone to care for her children. It was the biggest thing that had happened to Suzanne in years. And in that atmosphere of fun and faith and loving fellowship, her personality and sense of worth began to unfold and blossom.

"God loves you, Suzanne," they told her. "You are His child. He wants to do good things for you. He will help you build a better life for yourself and your family."

You should see Suzanne's family now. The kids are still full of life and bursting with energy, but the noisy and boisterous rowdyism is gone. They don't live in the Central Park housing project anymore. With help and guidance from a church counselor, Suzanne was able to move to a much nicer housing area. Instead of just sitting, she enrolled in vocational training to become a clinical nursing aide. How incredibly exciting it is to see her coming into church, dressed in her medical "scrubs" after work, looking tired but happy.

"God has brought me a mighty long way," said Suzanne. "I came back to the Lord as a result of these people showing love for my children. If they hadn't come to us, we'd never have gone to church. We were so far down that we couldn't help ourselves.

"Now I'm trying to encourage and help other people. Can you imagine that? I sure know what they're going through. The people of Without Walls kept telling me that God loved me and they loved me. After a while I started believing it, and it's totally changed my life."

We're somewhere in the future—looking much better there than we look right now!

Do You See
What I See?

"Isn't our new church beautiful? Just smell that new carpeting everywhere. And just listen to the choir singing! Do you see it? Can you hear it?"

We had moved out of the little storefront building after only a few months. People were swarming to our church from all over Tampa, especially from the public housing projects and the shabby streets of the inner city. Our congregation had a definite "vegetable-soup" appearance, with people of all colors, shapes, and sizes mixed together.

Even they must have thought I was a bit crazy when I started talking about new carpet and choirs. Our new "sanctuary" at the time was the cafeteria of a run-down public high school. Every Sunday morning, we had to go in early to move all the tables and chairs, clean up the mess of food spills and scraps, bring in all our equipment, and set up the chairs. After service on Sunday night, we had to move our stuff out and reset the tables and chairs.

Everyone soon learned that every fifty-five minutes a bell would ring, which during the week marked the beginning of class periods.

Without Walls

So right in the middle of worship, or the sermon, or the altar call, a loud bell would blare out a startling interruption. I never got used to it.

We'd received permission to rent the building from the Board of Education, but the school principal resented our being there. If we went five minutes past our allotted time in the evening, he'd start flashing the lights on and off. Invariably this would happen during a powerful move of God when the Holy Spirit was ministering to people with great spiritual hunger and need.

On occasion, we had week-long evening meetings in the school cafeteria, which meant sometimes there were school functions going on in the building at the same time. The wall between the cafeteria and the main corridor was made of glass, so students and parents would walk past and look in to see what we were doing. The congregation was seated facing the glass wall, so the people were continually distracted by kids out in the hallway making faces, copying what people were doing, and mocking the preacher.

In times like this, rather than getting irritated or upset, I'd start talking about hearing our choir singing and our orchestra playing—at the time, we didn't have any musicians or instruments. Or I'd describe the comfortable seats and the smell of fresh, new carpeting in our own building. It was a wonderful antidote for the frustrations and inconveniences.

The monthly rent for the school facility was two thousand dollars. At first we didn't have that kind of money and wondered how we'd ever manage. But I sensed God telling me to trust Him...that He would provide. Every single month, I didn't know where the money would come from until the last minute. But we were never late in paying our rent.

How could a church possibly grow in such adverse conditions? We had the wrong circumstances, a bad location, an undesirable environment—all the church-growth experts would tell you so. But our growth never stopped. We had one hundred seventeen people on our first Sunday in the school cafeteria, and the number increased for every service. I believe God put us in that place deliberately to show us His power and remind us that nothing is impossible with Him.

At about this time, we invited a guest preacher to speak for us. He was a very respected man of God who sometimes ministered in the area of the prophetic. On the Sunday he was with us, he prophesied over Paula and me and our congregation, two penniless young people and a ragtag handful of poor people in a rented school hall.

"God has called you to this city," he said. "Not only will you take this city for Jesus, but God has called you to the state, to the nation, and even to the world." The words we were hearing seemed impossible, but I sensed an awesome, supernatural significance to the message. The minister continued, "God has called you to be a training center to the world, to train and equip the body of Christ to evangelize this world. Men of great leadership stature will come minister from this pulpit—you will stand in awe at the caliber of people who will come. God will call people from the four corners of the world to relocate and be part of the work He is establishing. Men and women will come and lay down riches at your feet to help make this great work possible!"

Nothing magical happened after those prophetic words were spoken. Paula and I were still two young pastors, long on vision and short on resources. Our world-class outreach that was prophesied to reach the nations and shake the world was still a handful of needy people meeting in a run-down school cafeteria. So all we knew to do was to roll up our sleeves and go to work with renewed passion.

We began evangelizing in the community every Saturday. A nearby bakery had called to ask if we ever had a need for baked goods. We said, "Sure, we can use them." So they sent over truckloads of day-old bread and pastries. We took it into the public housing projects we'd been trying to reach and gave free food to people who really needed it. But we still had more bread and cakes and cookies, so we began going door to door, introducing our church, sharing Jesus with people, and blessing them with baked goods. We discovered a whole hidden population of widows, elderly people, and shut-ins whose health didn't allow them to get out of their houses. We began visiting regularly to minister to them.

The church never stopped growing. In addition to poor and

needy people, God sent some solid, middle-class working families who began to catch our vision. A couple who were very successful in business began to attend and to support the work. We taught everybody, street people and business people alike, what the Bible says about tithing—paying 10 percent of their income to the local storehouse, or church.

Week after week, our attendance increased and our financial needs were met. But conditions in the school got worse and worse. As we grew and needed more space, more chairs and additional rooms, the principal grew increasingly difficult and critical. Instead of the lights being flashed at ten o'clock, the "get-out" signal came at 9:45, then 9:30 . . . then nine o'clock. We knew that soon we would have to move.

When God wants you to move on, He makes it known by shaking you out of your comfort zone. Like a mother eagle stirring up her nest to uncover the thorns underneath, God nudges us over the edge to let us know it's time to fly. In our case, after we'd been meeting in the cafeteria for seven months, the school served notice on us that we had to leave—in one week!

The only place
where success
comes before work
is in the dictionary.

Confounding the Church-Growth Experts

The eighty-thousand-square-foot warehouse had sat empty for three years.

Well, almost empty. The homeless had been sleeping there, along with the birds and assorted small animals that are neither appealing nor friendly. The inside of the building was filthy, filled with trash and litter—a complete mess.

In fact, the property was in bad condition outside and in. There was no air conditioning, no ceiling, no inside walls. The floor was rough concrete, stained and dirty. To be usable for church meetings, partitions would have to be erected to enclose a fourteen-thousand-square foot sanctuary, a platform built, carpet installed, chairs hauled in and set up. The place needed additional lights, a sound system, rest rooms, and dozens of other details to be worked out.

Our church worked out a deal for the building on Tuesday. We intended to worship in our new church by the next Sunday!

Where do you move a church when you've outgrown a storefront building and had your lease canceled on a high school cafeteria? We hadn't been able to find anything anywhere in our price range.

But we didn't let financial considerations stop us.

I felt God was directing me to the south end of Tampa. When we drove into the area, we seemed to go directly to a huge warehouse in a run-down area. I knew it was the place. I could hear the voice of God saying, "This is going to be your building. Make an offer on it."

At that particular time, buildings in industrial areas were renting for about eighteen dollars a square foot. Even this building, in its poor condition, was worth a minimum of ten dollars a square foot. We made a ridiculous offer of about twenty-five cents a square foot on a three-year lease. The broker laughed and said there was no way in the world the deal would go through. But to his surprise, the owner called back and agreed to our terms.

Now all we had to do was clean up the space and make it usable...in less than five days. We started calling all the people who had been attending our services to let them know where the church would be meeting, and we asked them to come and help clean up the building. We took all the money the church had to buy materials. Someone donated ten thousand dollars for the project. Individuals and businesses donated lumber, carpet, and other supplies.

We started cleaning out the building, then laying out the new inside walls, painting, and putting up lights. By Friday the new church was starting to take shape. Many of us had been there for three days and nights straight, without even going home. But it was a labor of love. Somehow, some way, we were going to have a place for our church to meet by Sunday.

On Friday afternoon, as we were working, the real estate broker walked in. When he saw the work that had already been done, a look of horror swept over his face. He asked to speak to me right away.

We stepped away from the other people. Clearing his throat nervously, he said, "Reverend, we have sold the building."

"What? How can that be? Are you sure?"

"Well," he said, "I don't have the final papers, but it's as good as a done deal. Someone is buying it for a million dollars. You've got to stop all the work. I'm sorry, but you'll have to get out right away. The new owner wants to use the space."

I was devastated. That building had sat empty for years. Now, after we'd poured almost forty thousand dollars and countless hours of work into major renovations, it was being taken away! Sick at heart, I told the people what was happening. I went home to pray, and they stopped working and knelt down in the building to pray.

At home, I threw myself down and began to cry out to God. After a while, the Holy Spirit began stirring inside me, directing me to a promise found in Psalm 121:3: "He will not suffer thy foot to be moved...." I jumped up, washed my face, and hurried back to the warehouse.

"Okay, people. Get back to work! God has said, 'I will not suffer thy foot to be moved.' So this is our building." And we resumed the construction work. No matter how discouraging the situation seemed in the natural, we knew God was going to make a way.

Later that evening, the broker called me again, in total confusion. "I don't know what is going on," he said. "This was a done deal, but they have backed out of buying the building. Instead, they are buying a more expensive warehouse with a lot less space located just a block away. I don't know how this happened, but the building is still yours."

About thirty-six hours later, on Sunday morning, a tired but happy group of people welcomed the rest of our church congregation—and many visitors—to worship in our own building. It wasn't fancy. There was much work left to do, but nobody seemed to mind. We had a great day of celebration and rejoicing for what God had done. Now we had a place where we could spread out and grow.

Perhaps some churches that had grown as rapidly as ours and had finally moved into their own large building would have settled into a comfort zone. While we were thrilled to have this new facility, from the first week we recognized that this building was not a place to shut ourselves into, but it was a place of preparation for going out into the community. It was merely a training station, providing the space for different activities necessary to carry out our mission.

Our church confounds the church-growth experts. Everything we do—opening churches in storefronts, badly located schools, warehouses, tents—contradicts the traditional rules for growing a church. We've been told we couldn't build a church with poor people—that ongoing outreaches into the inner city were not viable without the strong financial support of outside organizations. But God has continued to increase and multiply our congregation. In 1993 and 1994, Dr. John Vaughn of Church Growth Institute named us as the second fastest-growing church in the nation. The next year we were named the fourth fastest-growing church.

How have we kept growing and kept having the provision to reach those who can give nothing in return? The Bible says, "Pure religion and undefiled before God and the Father is this, To visit the fatherless and widows in their affliction..." (James 1:27). Even when it seemed impossible, we ministered to the poor. And as we have followed the heartbeat of God, doing what He has asked us to do to help the needy, His blessing and supernatural provision have always been there in everything we have done. As we've ministered to the poor, God has brought us people of means and substance who were willing to share and be good stewards of their prosperity.

"How does it work," we're asked, "having Asians, Hispanics, South Africans, African Americans, and Caucasians all assembled together in a local church setting?" Or, "What do you mean you have the homeless, poverty-stricken, professional athletes, doctors, lawyers, and business people all worshiping together?"

My answer is that we are all washed in the same blood of Jesus Christ, and it is the blood that unites us as one. The devil will be confounded when we reach out to all men, no matter the color of their skin, their socioeconomic background, their education, or their heritage.

The ground around Calvary is level, equal for all. There is none righteous, no, not one! Christ the Savior would not be needed if we could straighten out our own lives. But we can't. So God loves us in spite of our sins, our bad habits, and our shortcomings. He says, "Come unto Me with all your junk, all your baggage, all your mind-sets, and I will wash you whiter than snow."

After He does that for us, we have no choice but to love other needy sinners around us. It's our job, then, to love the despised and forgotten, the "down and outs," the "up and outs," the winos and the social drinkers, the drug addicts and alcoholics, the prostitutes, homosexuals, the sick and wretched. Whoever we are, wherever we are, there is someone for us to reach. Revival can happen. Deliverance can come. Restoration is possible. God is willing and able. But we must help make it happen by being instruments of His love.

In Jesus' day, it was His
will to heal lepers.
Today it is His will to
heal AIDS.

Healed of
AIDS

G reg started coming to South Tampa Christian Center with his mother when the church had just begun and was meeting in the storefront. But after only a couple of months, Greg dropped out, having fallen back into the gay lifestyle that had plagued him since he was sixteen years old.

Greg's father had committed suicide, shooting himself in the bedroom. As a seven-year-old child, Greg was the one who found him. He felt rejected and abandoned by his father, deprived of the love he so desperately needed and sought.

By the time we met Greg, the HIV virus he had picked up years before had progressed into full-blown AIDS, and he was beginning to battle a variety of related health problems. Paula and I ministered to Greg, praying and counseling with him, explaining the scriptural teachings against homosexuality but stressing God's love and acceptance of him as an individual with great value and worth.

Greg's mother is a great woman of God. Through the years, she has prayed for her son, loving him and accepting him, while constantly urging him to commit his life completely to the transforming power of Christ. Beverly also has been actively involved in Liberty Ministries, an on-the-street outreach to the gay community that is supported by Without Walls.

For a dozen years or more, she went out every Friday and Saturday night to the gay bars and witnessed to the men there. "Jesus loves you," she told them. "He wants to be part of your lives." She never condemned them, never argued with them. Through the power of love alone, she earned the right to witness. Over the years she has won hundreds of these men to the Lord.

Beverly had the philosophy that if she wanted her son saved, she had to do more than pray. So she sowed love into the gay community and served them as best she could.

For years, Greg had one foot in the church and one foot in the gay culture, bouncing around back and forth, by his own admission pretty much playing games. He kept dabbling in the gay lifestyle, somehow feeling he'd be okay because his mother and the church were praying for him. But his health continued to deteriorate; on at least four occasions he came to the point of death with double pneumonia and an AIDS-related condition called Giardia, which involves a parasite that attacks the intestines, liver, and kidneys.

During the fourth attack, the medical staff at the Catholic hospital where he was being treated didn't think he was going to make it. He weighed only one hundred eleven pounds, and his T-cell count, which is about twelve hundred fifty in a normal person, had plummeted to seventeen. There didn't seem to be any hope, and the last rites were administered.

That night the Lord woke me up and laid Greg on my heart. As I prayed for him, I felt impressed to go to the hospital and tell him that this was absolutely his last chance—that either he turn his life over to God without reservation and be restored, or his life would come to an end.

So I did what God had directed me to do, and a barely conscious Greg nodded that he understood. I prayed for him there, and to everyone's astonishment, he rallied and began gaining strength. In a short time, his T-cell count went from the almost-fatal level of seventeen back to one hundred fifty-one, and at last report it was still climbing.

Greg has been consulting with his mother and other workers in Liberty Ministries on how to reach and counsel the homosexuals out on the street. He is also being asked to speak at some Christian conferences about ministering to the gay community.

"The only thing that will reach gay people is love," says Greg. "The only answer is the absolute, true love of God expressed through His people. Condemnation and a 'stay-away' attitude is very destructive. Pastor Randy and Pastor Paula and the Without Walls people just opened their arms and their hearts to me and said, 'We love you, and we're here for you.' And Pastor Randy had the courage to confront me with God's ultimatum when I was just a heartbeat away from death.

"I don't know how long the Lord will leave me here. I just try to live every day for Him as if it were my last day. My prayer is that God will use me to reach and help others in the gay lifestyle to accept the love of the Father they're really looking for."

Give a man a fish, and he'll eat for one day. Teach a man to fish, and he'll have food for a lifetime.

Table in the Wilderness

Do you know anybody who could use some turkeys?" What a question to ask a man who is building a "church without walls." I was having my hair cut, chatting with the hairdresser about some of the exciting new outreaches we were launching at the church. The man in the next chair had been listening for a while, and he took advantage of a lull in the conversation to ask his question.

Turning toward me, he said, "Here's my card. I'm the president of a food broker company. We usually sponsor the food for one big event each year. It sounds like you do quite a lot of work with needy people, so if we can help you, give us a call."

One of the constant challenges in working with the poor is finding the resources to help them. There are always plenty of needs. As Jesus said, "For ye have the poor always with you" (Matt. 26:11). And the desire to help and do good may be there almost always. But if the helper does not have the means to meet the need, there is little he can do.

So early on I learned to keep my antennae up and my ears open for supplies that could be channeled to hungry, hurting, and needy people. Now, here in the week before Thanksgiving, a man whose business is distributing food wants to know if I know anyone who could use some turkeys.

"I'll be calling, you can count on that!" And I did. That man's company donated a hundred large turkeys, along with a pallet of vegetables, stuffing, bread, and other things we needed to prepare Thanksgiving dinner for thousands of poor people. We decided to call the project "Table in the Wilderness," from Psalm 78:19.

We sent turkeys and fixings home with all our church members to cook and bring back to the church ready to serve. After we had cajoled everybody we could find to help cook, there were still turkeys left. So we began calling restaurants and explaining our situation. Many of them offered to cook turkeys for us.

At the time, the church only had two buses, but the school board joined the project by providing three buses and drivers. On Thanksgiving, all day long those five buses went back and forth, bringing homeless and needy people from every corner of the city to the church to join in the feast. We found them outside labor pool offices, under bridges, in social agency shelters, at The Salvation Army, and in the bleak area called "Suitcase City," where people gather who can carry all they own in one battered suitcase or shopping bag. At our "Table in the Wilderness" dining room, every person was invited to eat as much as they wanted, with second and third helpings of everything.

Once the meal was over, we invited those who needed clothing or shoes to our giant clothes closet. It was a great day. We went through a mountain of food and almost emptied our clothes closet as some fifteen hundred underprivileged citizens of our community joined us for Thanksgiving that year.

Since then we've welcomed as many as five thousand to our Thanksgiving "Table in the Wilderness." Each year we're never sure where the food and clothing will come from to share with those who so desperately need it. And every year, in some miraculous way, the food is provided.

I believe that if we work as if everything depends on us and pray as if everything depends on God, wonderful, miraculous things can be accomplished. When we really give our all to do what we can do, then we can expect God to do what He can do. And that's always more than enough.

ROAD TO RECOVERY

About this time, we launched an ambitious new outreach ministry we called the "Road to Recovery." It was based on the well-known premise that if you give a man a fish, you feed him for one day. If you teach him how to fish, you feed him for a lifetime.

We could see that no matter how many homeless people we fed on Thanksgiving, they were still homeless and hungry the next day. Giving alms to the poor is commendable and good, but it is not the answer. Federal and state welfare programs have proven that. We realized that, to make a real difference, we had to provide total care for the homeless.

We set out to locate and use all the resources we could find to help take the homeless out of hopeless situations and give them a chance to make it. Instead of providing just a handout, we wanted to give them a hand up to becoming productive Christians and contributing members of society.

To really help the homeless and poor get on the "road to recovery," we could see that we had to help them with jobs, houses, job training, and education. Yes, they often needed food and clothing to get started. And we found ways to provide it.

We started small, but the need was so great it was hard not to spread ourselves too thin. Before long, we had a dentist providing dental care, a doctor giving medical treatment, and a professional employment specialist helping find jobs.

The program was gratifying but exhausting. If any outreach is to be successful and continue to function, it must have dedicated, resourceful leadership. It's much easier to mobilize a group of people to launch a program than to find the key man or woman who will take over the responsibility to keep it going.

As we were starting our Road to Recovery program, God sent a special woman to the church. At one time in her life, Karen had felt a definite call of God on her life, but she had been discouraged by people telling her there was no place for women preachers. When she came to Without Walls, she immediately felt comfortable and knew this was the church for her.

Not long afterward, I announced that anyone who felt a call of God on their life should come to a class I was going to start teaching on how to find and function in the work God wants you to do. Karen felt she should attend, but she was hesitant because of the prejudicial views she had been taught about the place of women in the church. When she told me how she felt, I told her she needed to attend that class. The sessions provided a dramatic turning point for Karen as she discovered her gifts and calling for evangelism.

After a while, we chose Karen and her husband, Pat, to run the Road to Recovery ministry. Pat had retired from the military, and both he and Karen felt a special love for and calling to the homeless. We put them through our Master Pastor Internship Program, and they immediately began going out on the streets to share Jesus and build relationships. They provided food and clothing but also the Word of God. And they have seen extensive and dramatic results.

For example, three of our ushers at Without Walls are men who went through the Road to Recovery program. Formerly they were both "broke" and broken, without hope. Now they handle the church's money as they help take up the offering! Today they are productive Christians and citizens, with good jobs and comfortable homes. They are faithful tithers and givers to the church. That's true evangelism and restoration!

How can such a miraculous transformation take place? Through the grace and power of God, of course. But also because real believers stepped out of the four walls of a church building and did all they could to make a real, practical, measurable difference in someone's life.

Progress always requires
you to get out of your
comfort zone.

If It Were Not for Without Walls, I'd Be Dead by Now

By the time Steve shakily climbed on the blue church bus with a bunch of other homeless people to go to the morning service at Without Walls, he was almost literally on his last legs.

He hadn't eaten in days...or had a bath or changed clothes. He had no money and hadn't been able to scrounge up any coke to smoke. He felt terrible—weak, sick, deathly tired, and too depressed for words. Steve actually thought he might not make it through the day. "Better to die at church than out on the street," he thought grimly.

But he didn't die that day. The bus dropped its care-laden cargo at the church's feeding center, and Steve joined the others in getting coffee, juice, and some breakfast—but he was almost too sick to eat. However, the little he did get down made him feel a little stronger.

Then he made his way over to the "super dome" tent for the service that was already getting underway. The music and singing, the smiles, and the special "presence" he felt there began to lift his spirit. "I've sure made a mess of my life," he muttered under his breath. "Is it too late for me to change and get straightened out, Lord?"

The first thing I said when I took the microphone that morning was, "It's never too late with God! It doesn't matter how far you have fallen or how lost you have been; He still loves you and wants to lift you up, bring you back, and restore you to wholeness and new life. And you don't have to wait until you qualify or deserve His love. He'll do it for you right now!"

Steve heard those words as they were intended—straight from the heart of God directly to his ears. He nodded his head and said aloud, "It's a deal, Lord. I sure do need You."

After the service, Steve and the other homeless friends who had ridden the bus with him went back across campus to the feeding center to get some clean clothes. He was especially glad to get a pair of socks to make his feet more comfortable. Steve noticed and appreciated that the people on the ministry team were kind and loving, treating each individual with respect and dignity. Amazing—most people who passed them on the street treated them with disdain or open contempt, as if they were trash.

By the time lunch was served, Steve was beginning to feel like a new person, and he was able to enjoy eating the simple but nourishing meal. *Somebody does care what happens to me,* he thought. *God knows where I am, and He's taking care of me!*

Steve never did cocaine again from that day. "God took it off of me," he says. That's quite a statement, considering that drug abuse is what had ruined his life and dumped him in the gutter. When he was working, he'd spent most of his pay on drugs—four hundred to five hundred dollars a week. When he lost his job, he sold his furniture and television set to buy coke.

A native of the South, Steve had gotten involved with a woman several years before. She had a drug habit and got him hooked with her. "I messed up my marriage because of this woman—it was all my fault," said Steve. "It cost me my wife and my family, and the drugs took everything else I had, including my self-respect. Twice I even ended up in jail with some rough, rough guys. Only the mercy of God kept me in one piece.

"When I got involved with this other woman, I cashed in a ten-thousand-dollar insurance account I had and moved to Florida with her. I spent every penny that was left of that money on drugs and liquor. Things sort of went downhill from then on."

But after his spiritual encounter at Without Walls that Sunday morning, God began turning Steve's life around. His drug habit miraculously broken, he could begin to function again. A jack-of-all-trades, he found jobs painting, doing electrical work, repairs, and general maintenance. His earnings helped him eat and take care of himself.

Steve also began attending church regularly—in fact, he was there every time the doors were opened. And after several months, he was hanging around the church all the time. If the buses needed washing, he did it. If a truck needed to be unloaded, he took care of it. If help was needed in the kitchen to prepare meals for the homeless, he volunteered. If someone was needed to clean up the dining room, or wash dishes, or drive a bus, Steve was ready and willing.

Someone provided the funds to help him move into a mobile home of his own, and he began to get enough furniture and clothes to get by. For more than three years, he spent every spare minute at the church working with the homeless. He talked to the people, shared his testimony, and offered encouragement and a helping hand. Steve became a great blessing to everybody.

Steve now lives in another city. He owns his own mobile home and works as a painter. But he is actively involved in a local church, maintaining the building and grounds and working with the pastoral staff in the outreach programs. "I'm back out on the streets again," he said, "but not as a homeless person. Now I'm ministering to the homeless and helping lead them back to the Father's house. I'm so grateful to Pastor Randy and Pastor Paula and all my other friends at Without Walls who helped me get right with God. He is so good to me. Life is a joy now!"

The devil doesn't waste
stones on dead birds.

Sentenced
to Church

Frank was a long-haired, wild-tempered man who began attending our church after having many run-ins with the law. He had violated probation and was awaiting a court hearing when someone invited him to church. He was a broken, desperate man in need of a restoring God when he arrived, and the Lord immediately began to do a work of grace in his life. He volunteered to do maintenance work around the Without Walls office building; he also began going along with one of our outreach teams. As he tentatively began trying to witness to others and help them, God started doing a major overhaul inside him. Frank began to change, blossoming into a new creation before our very eyes.

The day came for his court appearance, and one of our staff pastors went with him for support. Frank was resigned to the fact that he probably would be returning to a cell after the hearing. His case was being heard by a man often called "the hanging judge," who had a reputation for being extra tough. On the day of Frank's hearing, the judge seemed anything but compassionate. One person who appeared in court that day was a mother with a baby in her arms. After hearing the attorney's arguments, the judge told his bailiff to take the baby from the mother. Then he sentenced her to jail. The gavel cracked down loudly. Then there was ominous silence in the room. What little hope Frank had tried to hold on to was snatched away.

Frank's case was the last one on the docket. The judge quickly and solemnly revoked his probation and ordered him back to jail to finish his sentence. As the officers came to put handcuffs on him and lead him away, the judge asked, "Do you have anything to say for yourself?"

Frank was extremely nervous, his hands trembling and his mouth dry. "Ye'…ye'…yes, Your Honor," he stuttered. "I…I…I have a letter from my pastor, if you'll please read it."

The judge opened the letter and read the few short paragraphs I had written. Looking up at Frank, he asked, "Do you attend Randy White's church?"

"Yes sir, I do. I am doing volunteer work and going on some outreach teams."

Strangely enough, the judge had never met me personally and had never attended our church. His only knowledge of our church was through secular television coverage of the special events we had conducted for underprivileged people.

"Well, in that case," the judge said, "I revoke my decision and order you to do your community hours under the church's direction and supervision. Our prisons are too full as it is."

So the order came down for Frank to serve the rest of his probationary time at the church. Evidently the judge sensed that this was a place of restoration.

And he was not disappointed. Frank successfully completed his probation at Without Walls church. He has recently married, and he and his wife are active members and participants in our outreach programs. Frank plays in our praise and worship band and is a clown for the children's ministries. Everybody loves him, and he loves everybody.

Isn't God good?

A little job done is better than a big job talked about!

If You Don't Put On a Program for Them, They'll Put On a Program for You!

Part of our success in developing outreach ministries has been our willingness to try something new. We never turn down any idea just because "we've never done it that way." Venturing into the unknown often leads to exciting discoveries...and sometimes drops you unexpectedly deep in never-never land. Either way, you learn something. And the ideas that don't work out can be pretty funny...at least, later.

One day two young staff members came to me all excited and enthused about doing a major children's event for inner-city kids. We'd never done anything like this before, so we didn't know what to expect. Michael, our youth pastor, and his wife, Vicki, who is director of our Operation Explosion outreach, were young in the Lord at the time, energetic and zealous, but also a bit naïve. But I approved their plan, and they worked hard to make it happen.

Michael and Vicki are very ambitious workers. They arranged for the fire department to bring over a fire engine to show the kids. They had an ice cream company send an ice cream truck, and there were soft drink and hot dog stands.

Without Walls

Our two church buses made trip after trip to the public housing projects, bringing loads of rough and unruly inner-city kids to the church. We filled up all eight hundred seats in the sanctuary.

For two hours, everything went surprisingly well. The kids played games, listened to music, and watched a clown. Then Michael spoke and gave an altar call, and scores of youngsters accepted Jesus as their Lord. It was wonderful!

But by now these eight hundred kids had been indoors for almost two and a half hours. So we dismissed them to go outside and enjoy the refreshments and entertainment we had provided. We expected them to go nicely and wait their turn. Instead, when the kids were unleashed, there was utter chaos and bedlam, with shoving, pushing, fights, screaming, and yelling.

We learned lesson one—never release eight hundred inner-city kids onto your property without being totally organized. Because if you don't have a program for them, they will put on a program for you. The workers we had recruited for the event tried desperately to get the youngsters under control, but there was nothing they could do. In a matter of minutes, all of them were so frustrated that they totally lost their cool...and the victory.

Then we learned lesson two. Deciding to end the event and get the kids home as quickly as possible, the workers started trying to group the kids by housing project. "All Central Park kids here...All North Boulevard kids here...All Rembrandt kids here...College Hill over here." Wrong! Call out bus numbers, if you must, but never territorial areas. Doing that only starts fights! And that is just what happened.

It was tough getting them loaded on the buses. And even after they got home, the kids were still so worked up they began to throw tomatoes and anything else they could find at the buses.

Lesson three was that while it's pretty easy to handle busloads of kids coming in, getting them home when you only have two buses is a king-size problem. What do you do with hundreds of kids who are left waiting in the "battle zone" until the buses return? It was a nightmare.

If it's true that you learn more from your mistakes than from your successes, that special event was a true learning experience.

Randy White

We didn't give up, and from the lessons learned that day emerged two of our most exciting ministries that touch the lives of some eight hundred children every Sunday. Each week, eight buses bring about three hundred to four hundred youngsters from several project areas in the inner city to hear the gospel through our Kids in the Kingdom outreach. At the same time, we are ministering to about the same number of children who belong to our church members. These kids always look forward to the Bible lessons, games, and fun of Kids Explosion.

We've learned our lesson well. I'll guarantee that when the kids arrive, we always have a program ready for them!

Everything we do is for souls.

The Easter Egg Hunt Miracle

The message of the gospel never changes, but the delivery methods do. In our quest to reach more unchurched people for the Lord, we decided to conduct the world's largest Easter egg hunt. By the time we got the idea, there were only two weeks to get it done. We knew it would be a huge challenge. And it was. But it was so effective that we still remember and use the in-house slogan—"eggs = souls!"

That first egg hunt was a unique learning process. It also produced an unusual miracle—with a funny twist.

Getting the eggs ready was the first challenge. The only egg hunts we knew anything about were the ones we had done at our homes, using real eggs we had colored in little vats of dye. But we had grand plans to do it on a big scale. So Vicki, once again in her naïve enthusiasm, ordered lots of eggs. A truckload of eggs. Exactly twenty-six thousand eggs, to be precise!

Dozens of people from the church each took dozens and dozens of eggs home to boil, dye, and decorate. Hauling that many eggs back and forth was a logistical nightmare. You might even say it was not what it was cracked up to be! Some of the eggs looked a bit worse for wear even before it was time to hide them.

In addition to getting the eggs ready, we worked really hard publicizing the event, which was to be held in a high school football stadium. We handed out flyers in ten schools within a close radius of the stadium. And the excitement began to build as hundreds of children decided to come to the Easter egg hunt.

The big day arrived. Between twenty-five hundred and three thousand jammed into the stands. Our musicians led the crowd in a session of lively praise and worship music, and then I preached. At the invitation, many adults and children raised their hands and prayed the salvation prayer.

No one had been allowed to touch the eggs until the service was over. By then, the kids were eager to get on with it.

Now, the people organizing this event forgot to ask the obvious question, "What do thousands of children do with twenty-six thousand hard-boiled eggs?" They're pretty messy, and there is only a limited number any single person can eat. So, what's left to do with them? Obviously, throw them!

What was intended to be the world's largest Easter egg hunt quickly degenerated into the world's largest Easter egg fight! In a matter of moments, at least twenty-five thousand of the original twenty-six thousand eggs had been thrown, kicked, stomped, smashed, squished, or otherwise destroyed. And the crowd went happily on its way.

Those of us left behind began to panic. The football field had turned from green to yellow, with smashed eggs and shells matted and trampled into the grass. Our contract with the school included leaving the field clean when we had finished.

How do you clean up a mess like that? Rakes and brooms seemed only to make matters worse. We were sick at heart—maybe even to our stomachs! We didn't know what in the world to do. Fortunately, God had the situation under control. He had arranged for about two thousand members of a cleanup crew to come do the job the next day.

We held an Easter sunrise service in the stadium the day after the egg fight. I was in the middle of my message when a massive flock of seagulls flew over our heads and swooped down to the field. They began to eat the eggs, while screaming at the top of their lungs. No one could even hear me preach.

But that wasn't the worst of it. Then the droppings from the flying gulls began to fall on the congregation that had gathered there. Can you envision it? I'm trying to preach, sea gulls are screaming, and people are trying to dodge the droppings!

It was great! It was chaos! But when the sea gulls were finished, there was not a trace of egg left on the field.

Of course, you still had to watch where you stepped.

By the way, we've continued to have giant Easter egg hunts every year. We always call it "The World's Largest Easter Egg Hunt." We broke the record in the *Guinness Book of World Records* one year, then topped our own record the next year. Our last event featured three hundred thousand eggs and attracted seven thousand people. We have now outgrown the Tampa Convention Center, where we were for two years, and we are looking for a larger facility.

The World's Largest Easter Egg Hunt is reported and promoted by every single TV news channel in the area. City dignitaries, celebrities, National Football League athletes and cheerleaders, professional wrestlers, and a host of others come to help out. But we never forget why we're doing it. We always stress that "eggs = souls!" Each year the Easter egg hunt is our largest soulwinning event!

They're always fun and effective evangelistic events. But we learned a valuable lesson from that first time. Now we use plastic eggs filled with candy and a Scripture verse, not real hard-boiled eggs. So far we haven't had any problem with candy fights.

We have now helped churches in several other areas launch giant Easter egg hunts. The concept has worked well for them as well. A church in West Palm Beach, Florida, had a turnout of five thousand for their first egg hunt, and there were an estimated six thousand involved in a Daytona Beach, Florida church event. We also helped a church in Alabama launch the same program.

To God be the glory!

What you make happen
for others, God will
make happen for you.

Sitting Among Princes

Many of the people who make up the congregation of Without Walls International Church were once trapped in the snares of Satan, but they have been wonderfully touched by the loving hand of God and restored to a place of service. God, in His infinite mercy, has not only restored them, but He has exalted and promoted many to leadership positions. "He raiseth up the poor out of the dust, and lifteth up the beggar from the dunghill, to set them among princes, and to make them inherit the throne of glory" (1 Sam. 2:8).

The majority of our staff members have come from a variety of extreme situations. We have divorcees, an ex-welfare mom, an ex-rock musician, a single father raising a child from an unwed relationship, an ex-stripper, a man who lived in a homosexual lifestyle for years, an ex-bartender, an ex-drug dealer and user, and a man widowed at a young age. And our youth pastor came to us, not from seminary—but from prison!

I have watched God remake, refill, return, remold, redo, and replenish them. Their lives are illustrated examples of restoration.

They have matured under our teaching, and they have become our best teachers, preachers, witnesses, and evangelists. God reached into the miry pit of their lives and gave them "beauty for ashes."

It is really true that "God hath chosen the foolish things of the world to confound the wise...and base things of the world, and things which are despised, hath God chosen..." (1 Cor. 1:27–28).

The vision of restoration must capture all true believers. If it doesn't, the church will never take off its religious cloak and never stop saying, "You're not good enough; you're not dressed right; you don't have the right social standing."

Religious Christians are just like Simon and his pharisaic friends described in Luke 7. While Jesus was a guest at Simon's house, a harlot slipped inside. She knelt and began to wash Jesus' feet with her tears of repentance and dry them with her hair. Then she kissed His feet and anointed them with precious ointment. Simon and his friends were appalled.

"How could this man be a prophet?" they asked in their hearts. "If He'd known what kind of woman this is, He would never have allowed her to be near Him or touch Him."

But Jesus was the Son of restoration, coming "to save that which was lost" (Matt. 18:11). He came to restore people like that scarlet woman. If it had been up to the Pharisees, she would have gone on in sin, bowed beneath a spirit of rejection. But Jesus, moved with compassion for her need, said, "Thy sins are forgiven.... Thy faith hath saved thee; go in peace" (Luke 7:48, 50).

She left that place feeling loved and forgiven because she had been touched by someone with the heart of restoration. James 5:20 makes the message clear: "Let him know, that he which converteth the sinner from the error of his way shall save a soul from death, and shall hide a multitude of sins."

THE CHURCH IS FULL OF PEOPLE WITH SKELETONS IN THEIR CLOSETS

The ministry of restoration is not just for the unchurched, those in the depths of sin and degradation. It is also for those who are spiritually crippled and infirm, who sit in the pews of America's

Randy White

churches each week, broken and hurting.

All the Christians I've ever met are imperfect. From time to time they slip and fall or go astray. All of us make mistakes. The church is full of people with skeletons in their closets. As the apostle Paul declared, "There is none righteous, no, not one" (Rom. 3:10).

If we are to be a church without walls, we must understand that restoration is not just for those who have never been born again, but also for those who know Christ. No one, no matter who they are or what position they hold, is without the need of God's restoration power at some time or another. As the psalmist said, "The LORD is my shepherd; I shall not want... He restoreth my soul..." (Ps. 23:1, 3).

Paul admonished the church, "Brothers, if someone is caught in a sin, you who are spiritual should restore him gently. But watch yourself, or you also may be tempted" (Gal. 6:1, NIV). Do you regard yourself as spiritual and mature in the Lord? Then you should be busy restoring those who have fallen.

Someone said that the army of God often shoots its own wounded. Some pastors and leaders are still bound in legalism, prejudice, and skepticism. They won't use people who have "skeletons" in their closets. Ask Ezekiel what God can do with dry bones. When the precious, costly blood of Jesus comes upon those skeletons, the power of God restores new life!

Why should we be so vindictive and hard on those who have made mistakes? Don't kick them because they're down! Don't point an accusing finger at them as if their sin could never happen to you! If you are truly spiritual, go to them, put your arms around them, and embrace them with the love of Christ. As you do what you can to help restore them, the Holy Spirit will come and mend the broken pieces of their lives.

The heartbeat of restoration must pound in our chests if we are to reach out to heal our broken church and our broken world. There is hope for the hopeless and help for the helpless in Jesus. He came to show them a way out of their world of hurt and shame. He is ready to lift them up, trust them again, and give them a place of service in His kingdom.

Perhaps you have made some bad decisions and serious mistakes in your life, and the devil is working overtime to put you under condemnation. The God I serve is a God of restoration, not condemnation. The Bible says, "There is therefore now no condemnation to them which are in Christ Jesus..." (Rom. 8:1).

Don't let the devil torment you with guilt or shame about your past or about the bad decisions you've made. Allow the Holy Spirit to heal your pain and brokenness and draw you back to Jesus. He wants to give you abundant life.

God uses broken lives. He uses cracked vessels. Let Him use your life for His glory. He will take away your excess baggage and mend your broken heart. Let Him meet your needs and heal your mind and body. The outcome will amaze you. What do you have to lose?

If you will accept it, you can have it. What's the catch? All God asks is that when you are restored, you reach out to others and bring them out of their darkness into Christ's wonderful light. Jesus said, "Freely ye have received, freely give" (Matt. 10:8).

In Jesus' day, miracles happened on the streets, not in the synagogue. Is the church looking in the wrong place today for the demonstration of God's miracle power?

Saved to the Uttermost

He had everybody's attention the minute he walked in. He was tall and thin with a scraggly beard and a flowing mane of thick, black hair that hung down to his waist. Dressed in black leather biker gear, with heavy boots and a well-worn leather riding jacket marked with the distinctive gang "colors" of the notorious "Outlaws," his very presence created a certain tension. Yet there was a curious gentleness about him.

His name was Low Rider, a name given to him by his biker friends, and he'd just been released from prison. While behind bars, he'd read an article about our church in *Charisma* magazine and thought, *I wonder if these people would care anything about me?* So he wrote a letter, and we answered back. Someone from our correspondence department began writing regularly, sharing the plan of salvation, encouraging, and trying to be a friend. "Jesus loves you," he wrote, "and so do we!" The letters provided hope and spiritual guidance to this broken man who was crying out to God in his cell. Now, months later and out of jail, he'd come to find the people who—even by mail—preached and practiced the gospel of restoration.

We soon learned his remarkable story, how he'd been delivered from a life of corruption, hate, and violence. From his childhood, Low Rider's background and circumstances marked him for trouble.

When he was just two years old, his father caught him playing with a pack of matches he'd found on a table. To teach him a lesson, his dad held the little boy's left hand over a lighter until it was black and charred. He tried to pull his hand away, screaming, "No, Daddy, no, no, please no!" But he couldn't get loose, and the burn was so severe that he spent six weeks in the hospital.

The abuse continued throughout his childhood, and Low Rider ran away from home twice before he was three years old. But no one rescued him, and he kept being sent back. His dad continued his abuse, even when neighborhood children and parents looked on, afraid to try to stop the abuse.

When Low Rider was ten, he came home late for supper. His enraged father punched him in the mouth, knocked him down, and then began kicking him in the head and face, knocking out four teeth. Again, no one came to the boy's aid.

When he turned sixteen, Low Rider couldn't take any more. He persuaded his mother and his little brother to pack up and leave while his father was away on business. But as they were moving their things out, his father came home early. Angered at his discovery that they were attempting to leave, he suddenly pulled a .38-caliber revolver from his pocket and shot his wife through the head as the children stood watching.

Low Rider remembers his dad looking down at the body, then swinging around to point the gun at him. The boy lunged at his father, beating him with his fists and struggling to take the gun away. He managed to get it, and as his dad bellowed threats at him, he cocked the trigger and pointed the weapon at his father's head, intending to kill his persecutor. But at the last instant, Low Rider heard a voice inside of him saying, "No, son, don't do it." After a long moment of indecision, he uncocked the pistol and ran out of the house.

After that gruesome day, Low Rider's life continued to spiral downward in confusion and despair. He put on a hard outer shell, looking rough, talking tough. But it was all a front to keep from getting hurt again. Inside, he was confused, afraid, and hurt.

And his troubles kept getting worse. He later met the members of the Outlaws motorcycle club at a party, impressing them with his macho swagger and growling style. The president of the local Outlaws chapter took a real liking to Low Rider; eventually he invited Low Rider to join the gang.

During the probationary period, Low Rider discovered that he was expected to be part of criminal activities like stealing cars and motorcycles, carrying guns, selling drugs, beating up and abusing women, and generally terrorizing people everywhere they went. There was even talk of killing rival bike club members. After a few months, he knew the gang lifestyle wasn't for him, but a fellow Outlaw told him the only way to quit was to die!

Then the whole gang participated in a major drug deal, off-loading forty million dollars' worth of dope and narcotics from a ship and stashing it in a warehouse on the docks. It was a high-pressure situation, with everybody working feverishly, always looking over their shoulders, not knowing if or when the police would burst in.

Low Rider knew he had to get out before the next job. And as soon as he got the opportunity, he rode away and never went back. Two weeks later, he was arrested by officers of the Drug Enforcement Agency. They had been the "dealers" at the drug off-load, which had been a sting operation set up against the Outlaws.

So Low Rider went to jail, facing multiple charges and up to forty years in prison. That's when he met God. Broken and crushed, he cried out to God in his prison cell, and the Lord Jesus came to him there. During this time, the prison ministry team from Without Walls began ministering to him, helping him learn how to trust God and live for Him.

God is truly spectacular. He reaches into the miry pit and lifts people out of their despair and distress. Even if you "make your bed in hell," Jesus will come looking for His lost sheep. He wants to embrace the prodigal and bring him home. That's restoration. And that's how God works.

Low Rider is an effective leader in our congregation, serving in an outreach ministry called the Loyal Warriors Motorcycle Club, which reaches out to motorcycle gang members with the message of salvation and restoration. He is a gentle, loving servant who can relate to those who think they've gone too far and sunk too low. Nothing shocks or intimidates him, and he is faithful to share his personal testimony of redemption. One of his favorite verses—and mine—is Hebrews 7:25, which says, "Wherefore he is able also to save them to the uttermost that come unto God by him, seeing he ever liveth to make intercession for them."

There are four kinds
of people in your life—
adders, subtractors,
multipliers, and
dividers.
Encourage the adders
and multipliers.
Avoid the subtractors
and dividers.

The Without Walls Ministry Team

Without Walls International Church is not a one-man show or the private platform for Randy and Paula White. It is God's work—His church. We just have the privilege of being a part of it.

I believe God calls specific individuals to leadership, but the ministry is not one man doing it all. The ministry is not one man thinking up ideas, then trying to carry them out all by himself. The pastor cannot do everything himself, no matter how capable he may be.

The pastor's role is to make disciples—to teach, train, encourage, and enable those who come to Christ to become workers in the harvest.

When the New Testament church was born, according to the biblical record, "the Lord added to the church daily such as should be saved" (Acts 2:47). I believe He also sends staff members and team players He has prepared and called for specific positions when we obey the scriptural injunction to "pray ye therefore the Lord of the harvest, that he will send forth labourers into his harvest" (Matt. 9:38).

Long ago we learned that each new member God adds to our staff brings new, innovative ideas for reaching our generation with the gospel. This is why the number of different ministries operating out of the church has multiplied so rapidly.

One of the secrets of the growth and development of our ministries is that I am always ready to listen to anyone who comes with an idea or a vision in their heart. I began with a vision, and I am ready to give opportunity to others who have visions.

Everyone who comes to Christ has particular skills and abilities, no matter what background they come from or what color their skin is. Each one has valuable life experience and expertise in a certain field. They all have the potential to be extensions of the ministry. And as they begin to implement their part of the overall vision, they take ownership of that outreach and do whatever it takes to make it happen.

We've learned that hirelings do not last long. We've seen many come and go. The work is too tough and demanding. It's not easy working with baby Christians, changing their spiritual diapers, or staying up through the night with them when they have problems. Our kind of ministries offer no glamour or glitz—just long hours and dirt under your fingernails. So we look for people God has raised up, people who have been saved to the uttermost, those who have been restored from lives of ruin and desperation. The Bible says that to whom much is given, much is required. (See Luke 12:48.) They owe their everything to God, and they minister, not for prestige or position, but out of love and gratitude to Him.

There was a time when I had to try to do everything myself. But God has helped us grow so fast that I have had to build a multilevel staff and learn how to work with and through them. When I look around the conference table during our weekly staff meetings, every leader I see has an amazing personal story of deliverance and restoration. I am so proud of each of them.

Christians are like teabags. They're not worth anything until they go through hot water.

I'm Going to Touch You As You've Never Been Touched

In 1997, ninety-one couples whose marriages were so troubled they were going to get divorced canceled their plans! What happened? They attended weekly marriage seminars and some private counseling at the church without walls. And ninety-one times that we know about in that year, God healed ruined relationships and restored messed-up marriages!

The director of our Marriage Enrichment Ministry is a dynamic Hispanic named Juan. When he became a full-time staff member at the church, he brought pastoral experience, a Bible college degree, and special training and certification as a Christian counselor. His life before these achievements had been colorful, too. He was a Marine Corps Vietnam veteran and had a successful business career in the corporate world...and a two-thousand-dollar-a-week cocaine habit.

Juan started doing drugs during his fifteen months in Vietnam. When he went back home and started college, drugs were a big thing on campus. He tried a little bit of everything—smoking twelve to fifteen joints of marijuana a day, drinking two or three six-packs of beer, and snorting as much coke as he could get his hands on.

After graduation, he enjoyed quick business success, working for major corporations like Procter and Gamble, Colgate-Palmolive, and the Vicks Company. He married, and he and his wife had three children. But his travel and work schedule gave him little time to spend with them. And his growing income provided the money to buy more and more drugs.

After several years, Juan's long-suffering wife became a Christian and began praying for him. Concerned about his destructive lifestyle, she told him, "Honey, I can't change you. Only God can. But you have to be ready. When you get tired of living that way, just call on the name of the Lord Jesus Christ, and He will come and save you."

At the time, Juan rejected her message as so much heretical mumbo-jumbo. But he recognized that his body was deteriorating. He was losing weight and bleeding in various parts of his body. One morning he stumbled into the bathroom and was shocked at the pitiful figure he saw in the mirror. He sensed something inside of him saying, "What's it going to take for you to stop destroying yourself?"

Juan looked up and said aloud, "Lord, if You're hearing me, I want to make a deal with You. If You want me, take away these drugs." After he prayed, he didn't feel a thing—no thunder and lightning, no surge of joy, no warm fuzzies, nothing! And he still had the craving for drugs for the next few days.

"Well, God, I guess You don't want me," he said. "I'm still addicted to this stuff, and I can't get off of it by myself."

The next Friday night, after a long evening of partying himself into a stupor, Juan dragged himself to bed. About an hour later, he was awakened by a "presence" in the room, and he heard what seemed to be an audible voice. At first he thought he was hallucinating from all the drugs he had taken. But he felt stone-cold sober and awake. The voice said, "I'm going to touch you as you've never been touched before!" And a surge of heat began moving through his body. For at least two hours, he felt something going on inside him, in his body and his heart. There was a cleansing and a healing, an indescribable spiritual "high." Then he fell asleep.

The next morning when Juan awoke, the "high" was still there, and the presence within him directed him to do a deliverance service in his house, getting rid of the drugs and alcohol, rebuking every addictive substance in the name of Jesus. Juan awakened his wife to be a witness of what he was doing.

She was skeptical at first. "Come on, don't fool around," she said. "Don't play games with something so serious."

"This is no game," he replied. "God spoke to me last night." His wife began to cry, thinking that her husband had either gone completely crazy or else was radically saved.

She soon discovered it was the latter. Within a few months, Juan was in Bible college, then taking counseling courses. And he became as radical in his ministry to others as he had been in his business dealings and his alcohol and drug abuse.

Juan served another congregation as an associate pastor for seven years before a Without Walls staff member talked with him one day. For weeks he had been seeking God about his feeling that God was shutting the door at that church and was moving him on to another assignment.

When Juan and I met each other and shook hands, we both knew right away that he was supposed to be part of our team. Now, in addition to the marriage enrichment ministry, he also heads our singles ministry, family counseling, and the Pregnancy Crisis Center network, as well as doing hospital visitation and special assignments.

The brighter the light,
the more bugs you'll
attract.

Heal the Sick in Body, Soul, and Spirit

The two women burst through the door into the waiting room and rushed over to the receptionist. "Please, my friend has to see a doctor right away! She's in terrible trouble."

The friend, a young Hispanic woman, was obviously in great distress. She was bending over in agony, clutching her stomach with both hands, moaning and crying. Then she'd walk a few steps, sway back and forth, and bend over almost double. Her face was contorted, eyes tearing, nose running.

The receptionist calmly led the girl away from the curious and mildly alarmed eyes of the waiting patients out front, back to an examining room. Answering the unasked question, a strong, quiet African American woman standing at the door said, "I think she's in withdrawal, Dr. Combs—probably heroin."

Probably in any regular medical clinic, the examining physician would have taken one look, then transported the writhing, groaning patient to a hospital. But this was no ordinary doctor and no ordinary clinic. This physician was Dr. Bethany Combs, and the clinic was Operation Med-Care at Without Walls International

Church. An experienced, board-certified medical doctor, Dr. Combs asked a few questions, then brought in an intercessory prayer partner to join in "treating" her.

The patient revealed that since she was fourteen years old she had been deeply involved in Santeria, a form of witchcraft that combines elements of voodoo and Catholicism. She had no idea that her drug addiction and witchcraft were in any way related—in fact, she was shocked to learn that the Greek word for witchcraft is *pharmacea*.

As Dr. Combs counseled with the girl, the intercessor silently prayed. Then the patient said, "I understand, and I want to be free." So they prayed together, a simple prayer asking God to deliver her from the enemy's bondage, spiritual and physical, and to heal her body.

The girl was instantly set free. The pain stopped, her face changed, and the distress ended, not gradually but immediately. After a few more minutes of counsel and encouragement, the girl and her friend walked out, excited and smiling.

A native of Tampa, Dr. Combs had a large private practice in Miami and Key Largo. Then she became a Christian, and soon afterward she felt that she should move back home. She quickly became the medical director for a large company that operated medical centers serving the inner city.

About that time, she began to understand that bringing healing to people involved more than treating physical symptoms with medications—that true healing required dealing with the whole person—spirit, soul, and body. This development ultimately created problems for Dr. Combs on the job. Her company was adamantly opposed to her mixing ministry and medicine.

By the time they came to a parting of the ways, Dr. Combs had discovered Without Walls International Church and had accepted Paula and me as her pastors. As a member of the church, she volunteered part of her time to Operation Explosion, going out into the inner city on our big pink outreach trucks.

When she began seeking our guidance about what she should do in her medical career, Paula and I could see the Lord's hand at work. For months we had felt it was time for the church to offer medical assistance for the people to whom we were ministering. We just hadn't been sure how to go about it.

Randy White

We were able to set up a first-class medical facility as part of a "not-for-profit" Community Development Corporation. A health maintenance organization that cares for Medicaid patients provided the funding to build the center on the first floor of our multipurpose office building. The center is beautiful and well-equipped; it is staffed by Dr. Combs, a medical assistant, an administrative assistant, a receptionist-medical transcriptionist, and an energetic older lady who is both prayer warrior and the driver of the van that picks up patients from the inner city and brings them to the clinic.

A family practitioner, Dr. Combs treats young and old, men and women, insurance and cash-paying patients as well as those who have nothing. Like most medical centers, Operation Med-Care is busy all day long, every day. Although its regular operating hours are through the week, almost every Sunday some of the homeless who are brought to church are taken to the clinic for treatment.

The center's new mobile clinic is completed and certified, and we are now scheduling regular visits into the inner-city housing projects on Saturdays and evenings. We are reaching a totally different population segment. We're finding that some older people and young men who might never go to a doctor's office will walk up to a van if the mobile clinic is in their own backyard.

One of the biggest outreaches involving the medical clinic—and now, the mobile clinic—is our annual Back-to-School Bash. This program provides backpacks and school supplies for inner-city kids at all of our regular Operation Explosion sites. But equally as important are the pre-school medical checkups we provide. The school system requires that each student have all his or her immunizations and a basic physical examination.

With the mobile clinic, Dr. Combs and her staff can now provide this health-care service in each project neighborhood, so mothers don't have to ride the bus to take their children to the clinic. The medical team can examine and treat from one hundred fifty to two hundred kids a day.

Operation Med-Care is an exciting and productive outreach that helps carry out our church's objectives of evangelism and restoration. Every day when we open the door to patients, we are responding to the command of Jesus Himself, who said, "Heal the sick who are there and tell them, 'The kingdom of God is near you'" (Luke 10:9, NIV).

A little job done is better than a big job talked about.

Whatever Your Hands Find to Do

S adie had been married over twenty years when her husband was
accused and found guilty of molesting little girls.

She was devastated...emotionally destroyed. But despite the
public humiliation and the rejection by neighbors and former
friends, Sadie tried to stand by her husband through a mandatory
psychological treatment (which he resisted), hoping their marriage
could be reconciled.

During this time, the family's savings, resources, and property
were used up paying debts, living expenses, and legal bills. With the
husband still unable to hold a job in the community, the family was
forced to survive on welfare and live in public housing.

Finally a social worker told Sadie that if her children continued
to live in the same household with their father, the state would
remove them to a safe environment. "If they stay under the same
roof with him one more night, we'll take them for their own pro-
tection," the social worker said.

When Sadie temporarily moved the children to a friend's home,
her husband exploded into vicious wrath. The final unraveling of
their already ragged relationship took a few more weeks, but finally
it ended in a bitter divorce.

Then Sadie had more problems. She came from a religious world that said, "If you're divorced, you're damaged goods and cannot play an active role in the church. If you should remarry, it's even worse—you might not even be saved!"

I understood Sadie's dismay because I had experienced the same reaction from the church world when I went through my traumatic divorce. My personal experience of brokenness has made me more sensitive and responsive to the hurt of people like Sadie.

In the past, Sadie had played an active role in her church, often filling the pulpit of small rural churches for vacationing pastors or being the leader of church-related missions trips. After the divorce, she was left sitting on the sidelines. Her pastor even told her it might be best if she and her children moved away from the community, perhaps even out of the state. He'd heard there might be an opportunity in Florida.

So she cried out to God, "Are You through with me, too? I committed no crime, yet I've been treated like a gross sinner. I am guilty of no offense, yet I've lost everything, and all my friends have turned against me. I fought to save my marriage, but when divorce was inevitable, even the church turned its back on me. What's the deal? What am I supposed to do?"

God immediately responded to the honest cry of her broken heart. "I still love you, My child. I am still with you. I want you to do whatever your hands find to do, and do it with all your heart."

So Sadie and her children moved to Florida. And through a chain of circumstances, they found themselves getting involved with the outreaches of Without Walls. Pastor Juan, with his expertise in dealing with the legalities of marital and family problems, assisted Sadie in complying with the court orders for supervised visitation of the children by her ex-husband.

Dr. Bethany Combs, from the church's Operation Med-Care, helped Sadie through a frightening siege with suspected breast cancer. Although she had no money or health insurance, she received the best of care.

Sadie attended single's classes at the church to help rebuild her spirit, and she got plugged in to the worship team and the choir. In addition to her full-time job at a legal office, she also began working part-time at the Without Walls Call Center, praying and counseling on the phone with people who had called in for help.

Her daughter, who had suffered from the family's trauma, received the special educational help she needed at the church's academy, and soon she was involved in the youth group and in the clowns and characters costume ministry. Her son became interested in playing the guitar and being part of an award-winning band.

Sadie was determined from the beginning to keep her son and daughter together and to raise them as a Christian family. And although they were cut off from their friends and relatives back home, the entire Without Walls congregation is now their family. "My kids go home with Hispanic families, African American families, people from all walks of life," said Sadie. "They are loved and accepted—and so very happy. We belong here.

"God is prospering me and my family, too. We're certainly not wealthy, but in a matter of months now, I'll be debt free. My car will soon be paid for. And I believe that soon we'll be able to get our own house again. God is so good—He always makes a way. He has been faithful to me."

Who knows what God is
getting ready to do?

Let's Just Praise
the Lord!

Neither Paula nor I are musicians. In fact, even our "singing" is strictly in the category of making a "joyful noise." But we love music, and we love praising and worshiping the Lord.

In the first year or so when our church was meeting in a rented school cafeteria, sometimes I tried to help our people learn to dream and catch a vision for the future. I'd say, "Can't you smell the new carpet in our own building? Don't you hear our band playing and our choir singing?"

And just as soon as possible, when the church was about three years old, I felt the Lord leading me to find a music minister. A pastor friend in Atlanta told me about a young African American man named Jeremy, a tremendously gifted singer-performer who had the same denominational background that Paula and I did. So I put in a call to him.

I told him, "We need somebody to come and build the music department for this church." There was no choir, and we had only a couple of volunteers playing instruments. Jeremy promised only to think and pray about it.

I found out later that he didn't think he wanted a church job. He was traveling with a professional Christian performing group, traveling all over the country and overseas. They sang in some large churches, but mostly they performed for company conventions, like Amway and IBM. Jeremy loved to sing, and he hoped someday to make it to Nashville and work in the recording industry.

Having grown up in a very strict, rigid church environment, Jeremy was reluctant to make church work his career. At age seventeen, he'd fathered a baby boy out of wedlock, and he had taken his son to raise. In the church where he grew up, such an offense required the person to confess before the congregation and apologize. Then he was "sat down" for a period of time—removed from any active ministry during a process of restoration.

Jeremy had come to believe that many churches were more caught up in their own inner "politics" than in proclaiming the gospel and ministering to the lost and needy. He had not turned away from God, and he remained loyal to his denomination. But he felt more comfortable ministering and serving God outside the church.

On some occasions when he had contact with ministry groups, he'd overhear comments about his single-parent situation, or he would be asked to leave his child at home. So the last thing he was looking for was a church "gig."

Jeremy had said to the Lord, "If You show me a church that is truly doing what You said the body of Christ should do—one that doesn't have a lot of 'religious' games going on—I will consider it." Not long after that he got the call from me.

Jeremy made a couple of visits to Tampa, observing what we were doing in the community and our emphasis on evangelism and restoration. He was clearly more interested in the church's vision and practical approach to ministry than by our facilities and musical program—or rather, our lack of them.

Then he told me, "Pastor, I may not be the man for the job. I don't play the piano—I don't even read music very well. I'm young, and I've never directed a choir or a band. All I've ever done is just sing for the Lord."

"Well, Jeremy, I just need you to come in and lead my people in praise and worship," I replied. "Come and be just who you are. Minister the way you feel led by the Holy Spirit. Do the type of music you like to do. Be as creative and artistic as you want. I'm giving you a platform. Do whatever God places upon your heart to do."

So Jeremy came, and he and his little boy were welcomed with open arms. From the beginning, there was a special anointing on him to lead the people into the throne room of God. Praise and worship became even more sacred and meaningful as he encouraged the congregation to open their hearts and pour out their souls before God.

Before long, Jeremy came to me and said, "I want to start a choir."

"Yes, let's have a choir," I answered him.

Starting with zero singers—absolutely nobody—Jeremy began recruiting singers and training them to work together as a unit. Within a year the choir had sixty voices, and they produced an absolutely electrifying sound.

But this was no ordinary choir, formed from upper-middle-class people who'd had some music lessons and been around church music all their lives. This group was made up of people who lived in inner-city housing projects...men who had been living on the streets...single mothers...ex-alcoholics and druggies....the impoverished...people struggling with heartache and depression. These were people who were willing to use what they had—their voices—in ministry for the church.

Jeremy understood that he could not just assemble these folks and say, "Hit the note of C and let's sing." He became their pastor. He taught them, prayed with them, went to their homes, and visited them in the hospital. He got involved with their needs and problems, took an interest in their children. He loved them and earned their respect by being there for them.

When he stood before those people, they sang their hearts out for him, pouring all their faith and joy and hope into the music. And not only were they singing their hearts out for Jeremy—they were singing and giving their all in music to the Lord who saved them. You've never heard such a choir!

Next Jeremy said, "I'd like to add some instruments . . . get some brass players and a bass."

"Yeah, let's do that," I replied.

And from here, there, and everywhere, he found astonishingly good musicians whose hearts were right toward the Lord. He built an awesome band, with full percussion, brass, bass, and keyboards, capable of turning out professional quality sound.

Jeremy came and said, "I'm going to write some songs."

I said, "Write them!" And he did.

"Pastor, I'd like to make a recording of the band and choir."

"Terrific! When can you start?"

And soon afterward, he and the Fine Arts Ministry began work on the first of two top-quality CD/tape recordings of the band and choir in dynamic, high-energy praise and worship sessions. The recordings have been extremely popular.

"What would you think about us going out on a couple of tours?"

"Good. Do it!"

In addition to his outstanding work with the Fine Arts Ministry, Jeremy also is a gifted, compassionate counselor; he directs a special outreach for people twenty to thirty years of age—Focus on Young Individuals, or FYI.

Although a vital part of the local ministry and outreach of Without Walls, Jeremy has become a passionate visionary. Recently he spoke out on what he sees as the emerging role of the church. "I believe God is guiding us into an apostolic movement. There is such a need across the land for what Without Walls is doing. Too many churches are blind to the poverty and hurt around them. In many areas it is awkward and uncomfortable to have an interracial congregation. Lots of good people are just plain scared of the unknown—it's hard for them to let their walls down and build a bridge to the world around them.

"God is going to use Without Walls in a greater way to help other churches begin doing what we do here. It's not impossible. Any church that will be obedient to the Word of God can make a major impact on their community. I see the different departments and outreach centers of our church beginning to conduct seminars and discipling other churches on how to get people off welfare, how to reach the homeless, and how to minister to families in the inner cities. Our training centers can help others discover just how simple it really is to do the work of the Lord.

"For example, my music staff and I can teach other churches how to do praise and worship in the new millennium, how to grow a choir from zero to hundreds, how to minister to the hearts of the people. If it's working in Tampa, it will work anywhere. Who knows what God's getting ready to do?"

Small hinges swing big
doors.

My Feet Are Firmly Planted

Denise was headed for major trouble. She was going out a lot, doing drugs a lot, drinking every weekend. She was even into the "rave" scene, attending late-night dance clubs where the drugs of choice for everybody were "Ecstasy" or "acid"—LSD. The desired effect was to make the participants extremely sensitive to sensation—to touch and to feeling.

But the main thing Denise felt after the drugs wore off was incredible loneliness. As she described it, "I could be in a room with hundreds of people and be the loneliest soul there. I knew there was something missing in my life."

One of Denise's acquaintances began asking her to come to church with her at Without Walls. "No way," she said. "My parents made me go to church when I was younger. Now I'm doing lots of stuff the church wouldn't like, and I'm not ready to change yet. Maybe I'll go later on in life."

But the friend kept insisting to Denise that she "just come one Thursday night." Finally she did. Paula was speaking that night, and there was a powerful move of the Holy Spirit in the service. To her utter amazement, Denise felt the love of God drawing her and doing a work inside her head and heart.

She was hooked on a new high! She hardly missed a service after that. To her amazement, the lifestyle she thought would be so hard to give up as a Christian began to slip away. The rebellious spirit that had driven her for years lost its power. Bad language, smoking, and drinking stopped without her even trying to quit. The desire for drugs faded…and died.

Little by little, Denise saw changes taking place in her life. A counselor at church helped her realize that she had lots of anger, hurt, and hate built up inside toward her parents. When she graduated from high school, her mother left home because of spousal abuse. At the time, Denise had said, "Fine—whatever! I don't need either of you!" But bitterness nearly destroyed her. Finally the day came when Denise called her mother and said, "I just want you to know that I forgive you."

Talented and witty, Denise sings in the choir and works with Pastor Jeremy in FYI—Focus on Young Individuals, a ministry for people between the ages twenty and thirty. "There's always something going on around here," she said. "The Lord helps us find ways to really make a difference in people's lives. It's awesome. I love this church. My feet are firmly planted here. I wouldn't trade it for the world!

"One more thing. One Sunday Pastor taught about tithing and giving. I had never understood about tithing or giving money to the church. Pastor challenged everybody to plant a seed and give their best offering. I said, 'Look, I'm going to try this out, God.' And I gave more money than I ever thought I'd share with anybody. 'Here's my cash, God. I've got faith in You.'

"The very next day, on Monday morning at work, I was offered a new position that paid eight thousand dollars a year more than I'd been making! Plus, because it was a phone company, I also got free unlimited long-distance phone minutes. That might not sound like much, but when you're a twenty-two-year-old girl—that's amazing!

"I am so blessed! I can hardly believe all the neat stuff the Lord is doing in my life. God never ceases to amaze me!"

How do you eat
an elephant?
One bite at a time!

God Works in Mysterious Ways

Without Walls International Church has always been about people, not buildings. I believe the real church of Jesus Christ is comprised of the precious souls, redeemed and restored, that make up His body, not brick and mortar, stained glass and padded pews. Nice facilities are wonderful and vitally needed. But they are not the church.

A little more than a year after we moved into the warehouse, we were experiencing growing pains. We had long since stopped being a small church. In our first year, we'd gone from five people to about eight hundred. And the growth was continuing. There was still plenty of room in the building, but our ministry outreaches were exploding.

We felt led to have a banquet to present our vision and raise funds. We wanted to show the community what God was doing and the difference we were making in people's lives. Vice President Dan Quayle had agreed to be the special guest speaker at the event, and as he learned more about our "without walls" concept, he developed a deep interest in our work. Almost the entire city council, other prominent politicians, and many important business people accepted the invitation to attend our banquet.

Four days before the banquet, Vice President Quayle took seriously ill and was admitted to the hospital. His aide called to say he still wanted to speak if he felt well enough, but later—at the last minute—he had to cancel. Paula and I were just a bit panicky!

Clutching at straws, I placed a call to Pastor Benny Hinn, in Orlando, Florida. With his large church, television ministry, and citywide evangelistic meetings, I knew his schedule was always busy, booked weeks and months in advance. But he had been a great friend to us, and I felt strongly that I should ask him if he could help us out. "I have a few days open that week," he said. "I'd be glad to come."

The banquet was a powerful time of ministry. We gave a report of the various ways our church was reaching out to needy, hurting, hungry people, and our vision to reach and win all of Tampa for Jesus Christ. Pastor Benny spoke and ministered boldly and with great compassion. There was a beautiful response from the banquet guests to both the vision and the personal ministry.

One of the ladies who attended was a very wealthy lady from a prominent and successful business family. She was touched by what we were doing to help the poor and to meet practical, physical needs as well as spiritual needs. A few days after the banquet she sent a contribution of ten thousand dollars. We were grateful for her generosity, but we had no way of knowing that she would later be used of God to help bring about a great miracle of provision for the church.

A few months after the banquet, trouble began to emerge with our lease on the warehouse. We had a good credit history and a perfect payment record. We'd done lots of renovation and work inside to make the building really nice. In addition to having plenty of space for ministry offices and all our church departments and outreaches, the back of the building had been given over to a Drug and Alcohol Rehabilitation Center where sixty men were housed.

So we were shocked when the real estate broker who managed the property showed up one day and said they were going to lease out forty thousand square feet of the warehouse to another company. That was half of our space. How could they do this?

We still had more than a year to go on our lease for the space. Our contract also gave us the first right to purchase the property, which we'd always assumed we would do someday. Now, over our protests, the broker violated our agreement and rented half of the warehouse to someone else! We understood why, of course. We were only paying about twenty-five cents a square foot for the space, and the going rate was now between eight dollars and fifteen dollars a square foot.

It seemed that our only recourse was to take legal action, but as we prayed about it we didn't feel that was the thing to do. So we rearranged and consolidated our activity rooms and gave up the space.

In a few weeks, the broker came back and said he was taking another twenty thousand square feet. Although it was totally illegal, we could feel that an eviction notice was coming. We'd been squeezed from eighty thousand to twenty thousand square feet, and we no longer had enough room to operate.

We managed to rent some makeshift offices in a building across the street, but we were still cramped for space in the warehouse. Out of necessity, we moved our children's church outside into a tent. This kind of inconvenience did not disturb our church people as much as it did us. They were not coming to church because of the building, but for the love and acceptance they felt, and for the deep moving of the Spirit and power of God.

Paula and I soon sensed that God was allowing us to be put into this situation. Like the children of Israel in the wilderness who were led by the cloud of God's presence in the day and a pillar of fire by night, we sensed that when the cloud moves, it's time to go!

We started looking for somewhere we could move. There was nothing available that would meet our needs. Once we made a deal for a building that could have worked, but it fell through at the last minute. (Later the building sold for the same amount we had offered.)

One morning Paula and I decided to spend the whole day looking for a suitable property. We just drove around, looking and praying. We drove north. We drove south. We drove east. We drove west. We found nothing suitable within our price range.

Without Walls

The very next day, Paula was driving down Dale Mabry Boulevard when suddenly she heard the voice of God say, "Turn here!" She turned onto a road she'd never been on before, just a couple of blocks from Tampa Stadium. As she passed a side street, out of the corner of her eye she saw a boarded-up building that had been badly vandalized, with vines growing up the walls, weeds poking through cracks in the parking lot, and tall grass growing everywhere. There was no "For Sale" sign that she could see.

Paula drove back to the house and told me what had happened. Instantly I felt a quickening in my spirit that this was the building we'd been looking for.

Don't See Things As They Are but As They Will Be

When I saw it later, I wasn't so sure. There were no doors on the building, and many windows were cracked or broken out. The plumbing fixtures were broken or missing completely. There were no ceilings on any of the four floors. Thieves had stripped out the wiring to sell. Once a prestigious office structure appraised at $4.4 million, it was now a derelict hulk. Builders who looked at it told us it would take a minimum of $1.5 million to make it usable again.

But I still felt in my spirit that this was the location God wanted us to have. The building sat on six acres of prime real estate in a key location in the city of Tampa. I felt directed to make an offer of $1.4 million. The owner laughed at me and told me not to waste his time. "Call me back when you have a serious offer," he said. The offer I had just made was serious to me, considering that the church only had seventy thousand dollars in the bank.

In the natural, our situation looked hopeless. We took some of our church leaders and people to walk and pray on the office property, seeking direction from God. We all still felt this was supposed to be ours.

The owner didn't feel that way, though. The least he was willing to take was $2.5 million...in cash. That wouldn't work for us. Our congregation was only three and a half years old, and banks usually won't lend to a church until it has proven itself for five years. As an independent church, we had no denominational backing.

But somehow I knew God was going to give us this building. Every day we drove by the property and prayed. In the natural, all we could see was a broken-down building with grass and weeds growing everywhere. But I would say, "Can't you see how beautiful it will be with everything repaired and restored? Can't you just see the buses driving up, bringing the homeless and the people from the projects? Imagine all the new outreaches we can launch from this facility!"

We'd been able to get extensions on our lease at the warehouse, but the limited space we had was cramping our growth. With no place else to go at the time, we decided to wait and see what would happen. Weeks turned into months. Then a year passed. We still had found no other location that was right.

One day the Lord distinctly spoke to me to make our offer on the building again. So I went back to the office and called the owner's agent, expecting the same reply. To my surprise, he told me the building had been sold in an auction, one of hundreds of properties around the country that had been included in the deal.

I tracked down the company that had purchased all those properties. Soon I was talking to a manager, asking if he knew about a building on North Grady in Tampa, Florida. He chuckled. "That's really funny. I've got the title deed for that building right here on my desk. Would you like to make me an offer for it?"

The company didn't have an appraisal on the building—no one had even been to see it yet. As I breathed a prayer, I felt I should offer six hundred thousand dollars. Without a moment's hesitation, the man said, "Pastor, you've bought yourself a building. All you have to do is pay the closing costs and six hundred thousand dollars in cash in thirty days!"

The man faxed a contract, which I signed. I also sent a deposit of thirty thousand dollars. Talk about a step of faith! We didn't have the funds to pay for the building. We couldn't borrow the money. Our attorney was very concerned, knowing the deal couldn't go through without payment in full in cash. "Don't worry," I told him. "My Father is very wealthy. The money won't be a problem."

Soon he'd call again, still concerned. "Have you talked to your dad about the money yet?"

"Yes, I was talking to Him just today," I'd reply. "Don't worry. Everything is going to work out just fine." Like Abraham, I was determined not to stagger at the promise of God, "being fully persuaded that, what he had promised, he was able also to perform" (Rom. 4:21).

A week went by. Two weeks. No money. No financing. No prospects.

How Much Do You Need?

On the eighteenth day, I got a phone call from the wealthy lady who had attended our banquet months before and had sent us ten thousand dollars. She'd heard we were trying to purchase a building for our ministry. I told her that was correct. "How much do you need to get it—four hundred thousand dollars, five hundred thousand dollars?"

I told her how much was needed...and when. "All right, you've got it. I'll be there at the closing with a cashier's check." And on the thirtieth day, she showed up with six hundred thirty thousand dollars—enough to pay for the building, closing costs and all. The building was ours, debt free.

But that wasn't the end of the miracle. As it turned out, the lady's son was one of the original builders and owners of the building. She knew details and information about the structure that would be invaluable in repairing and restoring it for use.

By the way, it didn't cost $1.5 million to repair the building. Most of the work was done by the people of the church. This is what we call sweat equity. We did it floor by floor, cleaning, painting, installing new wiring, lights, and ceilings. We replaced doors and windows, put down new carpeting, and cut down the weeds and grass outside. We spent about two hundred thousand dollars for materials, paying for it as we went. It took a little over a year, but it was done debt free.

The building provides offices, a Christian school, a medical center, children's facilities, our Road to Recovery Center, Club X for teens, and our Bible college.

But we still didn't have an auditorium or sanctuary where the people could meet to worship. What were we going to do? Had God forgotten? Absolutely not.

The phone rang; it was an evangelist we had never met who didn't know anything about our need. "Pastor, God woke me up in the middle of the night and told me you need a place to worship."

"That's right. We're losing the place where we've been meeting. We have an office building, but no auditorium."

"Well, I have a large crusade tent, with a platform, sound system, lights, and chairs. It's ready to set up, and it's yours free for a year!"

"Bring it on," I said. "We've been waiting for you."

People advised us that it would be a fatal mistake to try and have church in a tent in South Florida. They said it would be so uncomfortable and inconvenient that the people would leave and never come back. "It's suicide to do that," they said.

Well, we worshiped in that tent for two and a half years. We sweated in temperatures over one hundred degrees. We brought blankets, gloves, and hot water bottles to stay warm through one of the coldest winters in Florida history. The tent withstood hurricanes with eighty mile-per-hour winds. It was struck by lightning.

Finally we replaced the canvas tent with what we called the "super dome." It was an inflatable, "balloon wall" structure, fully enclosed, air-conditioned, with carpet on the floor. And it was big, seating five hundred more people than the canvas tent in each service.

Through it all, the people kept coming. The church kept growing. Why? Because the people are the church, not the building. The people weren't fussy about our facilities. They just wanted to be where the anointing of God is.

Dream large, my soul,
dream large. God thinks
His thoughts through
you!

A "Hand Up" Instead of a Handout

Pastor, what are you going to do with those trucks? I've got an idea of how we can use them to bless people!"

When Without Walls International Church decided to use a big gospel tent for our sanctuary, we acquired all the equipment that had been used by a traveling evangelist. The canvas and poles, the platform and sound equipment, and the chairs all came packed in three big semitrailer trucks.

After we got the tent set up, the trucks were just sitting there. That's when Vinnie asked what my plans were for them. I really hadn't given it much thought. "What's your idea, Vinnie?"

"Let's use them to teach men a trade. We can take homeless men—guys just sitting around on welfare—and train them to be truck drivers," he said excitedly. "We'll give them a 'hand up' instead of a handout. Then they can get jobs and earn a good living. I've spent years teaching guys to drive trucks. I even went through special training to do Commercial Driver's License testing for the state. We could open an official state test site right here!"

And so we did. Vinnie had been an over-the-road trucker and

then a trainer-instructor for a large trucking company; he knows his stuff. He has the firsthand experience and qualifications to teach men how to maintain and repair their rigs as well as drive them. With his thorough, hands-on instruction, the church's truck driving school offers a three-week course in the basic fundamentals, including all the safety regulations, record keeping, driving, backing, and parking. So far, Vinnie has successfully trained some forty truck drivers at the church's school.

During the three weeks, Vinnie inevitably ends up answering some off-the-record questions for his students...questions about God, deliverance, forgiveness, and salvation. When they ask, Vinnie has an amazing personal testimony to share.

There was a time when Vinnie regularly grew ten acres of marijuana each year and sold it. He later became a virtual drug lord, buying cocaine direct from South America and selling it to large-volume dealers. He generously used his own product as well, becoming so enslaved to drugs that only a miracle of God could have saved him. He estimates that he was personally abusing at least two thousand dollars worth of coke a week.

But when he came to the end of himself and cried out for deliverance from the Lord, God cleansed his system of drugs and took away the addiction, the sickness, and the craving. Now Vinnie works as hard for God as he did for the devil.

His vision is to set up a system of vocational-technical training for inner-city people in a variety of trades. Using homeless and unemployed people to provide the work, he wants to refurbish houses and buildings in the inner city and then sell them. In the process, he will train people to be carpenters, masons, plumbers, electricians, and painters. He also envisions setting up a plant nursery, tending and operating it with inner-city trainees.

Vinnie reminds me of a line from a poem I once read that talks about having large dreams, because God thinks His thoughts through us!

Work as if it's all up to you; pray as if it's all up to God.

Victory Is Shouting in Our Neighborhood

In addition to church-operated ministries that are staffed and financed by Without Walls International Church, there are several tremendous community outreaches that share our vision and are affiliated with our church, but operate independently.

One such service is an employment assistance agency headed by Dave, which is known as VISION—Victory Is Shouting in Our Neighborhood, Inc. A nonprofit corporation, VISION seeks to help restore "at risk" neighborhoods through group counseling, personalized mentoring, and an aggressive program of employment services. This arm of ministry provides job placement for some five hundred individuals a year.

Dave had spent almost two decades working with secular nonprofit organizations that helped provide jobs for target populations—usually low-income, inner-city, minority youth and people with handicaps or addictions. And although a service provider, he was part of one of the "target" groups. Dave was an alcoholic and a crack addict.

How bad an addict? In Dave's words, "Every time I got my

hands on any money, I spent it all on drugs—probably four hundred to five hundred dollars a week!"

Dave had other problems, too. Not surprisingly, he wasn't getting along well with his wife, and he had some growing problems at work. But he felt powerless to change what was happening to him.

He and his wife lived in a neighborhood near Without Walls. Dave remembers hearing the music from the services; volunteers often dropped off leaflets and flyers advertising special meetings and upcoming events at the church. So they decided to give this unusual church that met in an air-suspended dome a try. From the first service, they both sensed a compelling anointing and felt a strong conviction during the preaching.

Then one Sunday right before Memorial Day, Dave found himself down front at the altar, doing business with God. He laid down his heavy burden and said, "God, I just can't carry this any longer. I can't keep up this drinking and doing all these drugs. It's too much to handle, so I give it all to You. Pastor Randy said You'd help me, so I'm counting on You from this day on."

From that hour, Dave never took another drink and never did cocaine again. God took away all the craving, the addiction, and the symptoms. Dave was even freed from smoking cigarettes. And he and his wife began to find a place to serve the Lord together in the congregation.

A few months later, in November, Dave lost his job. Although he had enjoyed a successful career, his job was just specialized enough that he could not find another similar situation. So he mentioned it to a friend at church who was a staff member and asked for prayer that he'd find a new position.

The friend said, "You know, we've been talking about finding a way to help unemployed people in the congregation find jobs. We might just be looking for someone with your background and training." And he set up an appointment for Dave to meet with me.

I was impressed with Dave's obvious desire to use his expertise in God's work. He really had a vision to help rebuild problem communities and restore the troubled, defeated people who lived in them with honest, productive employment.

"What is it you need to do this?" I asked him.

"Pastor, my business is finding jobs, so I'm not asking for any money from the church. I just need your help and encouragement to keep my life straight and my marriage strong. I need your support in getting my nonprofit organization set up and operating. I want to call it VISION—Victory Is Shouting in Our Neighborhood, Inc."

"You've got a deal," I told him. "Let's get started. Just let me know how we can help."

VISION, Inc. was set up, and three months later Dave excitedly told me that he'd received a sizable government grant through the state's Department of Labor and Employment Security. This funding would help him recruit unemployed people and get them regular employment in the workplace.

Dave is very talented in motivating and restoring confidence in people who have not been successful in the work force. His follow-up and ongoing support have helped hundreds of people—many of them longtime welfare recipients—become confident, productive workers who are proud to be earning their own way.

Many of his clients have come from the congregation of Without Walls, some from the community at large. On occasion he has been able to place successful trainees of the church's truck driving school program.

One lady who was in the church choir desperately needed a job. She was on welfare, with no skills. The only work experience she'd ever had was in very low-pay restaurants. Dave found her a position as a customer service representative for a parcel service. The company provided schooling and on-the-job training with computers, people contact, and delivery. She's doing great, and she has received three raises in a four-month period!

I don't know who's the proudest of that dear lady's accomplishment—she, Dave, or I! All three of us know that VISION really does mean that Victory Is Shouting in Our Neighborhood!

We have been driving by
the congregation to get
to the church—and
flying over the mission
to get to the mission
field.

So Send I You!

By 1993 the pattern of outreach ministry God had directed us to set up in Tampa to reach the city was well established and proving its effectiveness in reaching the poor and homeless of the inner city. The phenomenal growth of Without Walls was directly attributable to these Christ-centered ministries to the community.

It was time to share the principles God had given us with others, to see others take the plan and use it in their cities to reap a harvest of souls. We had the vision for operating an International Operation Explosion Seminar to share the techniques we had learned. But how were we to go about it? Who would come to a little-known church in Tampa to learn the principles of community evangelism?

If God directs you to do something and you say *yes* to Him, He will work out the details.

Paula was really the instrument God used in this situation. In a June visit to another Florida church that was experiencing a tremendous revival, she had a vivid confrontation with the Lord. Weary from the pressure and demands of our ministry, she received a

185

refreshing and rejuvenation from the Holy Spirit. After hours of spiritual communion, she heard the voice of God saying, "Ask largely." Knowing that the Lord was not referring to more money or a larger ministry, Paula immediately focused on reaching more souls.

"Lord, let me win fifty thousand souls for You before the year is out," she prayed. Although only half the year remained, she felt confident that God would honor her request.

A few weeks later, Paula attended a camp meeting in Louisville, Kentucky, where she encountered some friends who were active in overseas missions work. At dinner one night, they listened in amazement to her account of what God was doing to reach inner-city people—especially children—in Tampa.

The lady said, "We've lived in Los Angeles for twenty-five years, and we've never done anything for the children of our own city. Do you think what you've been doing would work in L.A.?"

Los Angeles had recently been overwhelmed by riots and violence in the streets. Tensions were high, and many were fearful that the city would experience ongoing conflict. Was evangelism and restoration possible there? The Holy Spirit moved inside Paula like an explosion going off. "YES!" she shouted, and she and her friend both began crying. The other patrons in the dining room began looking at them as though they were weird.

Within a few days, Paula and Vicki flew to L.A. to begin organizing a major outreach they called "Operation STITCHES" (Saving the Inner City Through Christ's Hope Eternal Salvation). They called on area churches to rally support, but they received no encouragement. "My advice for you is to go back home to Tampa," one ministry leader told them.

When Paula told one pastor that God had called her to come into L.A. and shake it with His power, he laughed and said it would never happen. But such doubts only increased the resolve of the team.

The news media found out about the plans for the evangelistic blitz and began to make fun of them. Some gang leaders sent death threats to anyone who came onto their turf. But the more opposition there was, the more people heard about the upcoming meetings and started getting interested.

Randy White

Before it was over, the same church leaders who had scoffed at the proposed inner-city crusade got their congregations involved in what was to become a citywide outreach called "Hope for L.A." So the rallies and meetings took place—right in the heart of the riot areas where most people had been afraid to go. "Operation STITCHES" took its big rolling sanctuary trucks into the Nickerson Gardens and Jordan Downes neighborhoods of Watts, as well as to Alisio, Pueblo Village, and Wivenwood. At least one thousand people showed up at each site. God worked great miracles in those meetings. Short limbs grew out instantly, cancers dried up, and there were other outstanding healings. One night there were three hundred Spanish-speaking mothers in the service, but we had no interpreter. Miraculously, those ladies testified that they understood every word. There were some tense moments during the crusade, but the love of Jesus prevailed over every threat. And peace came to L.A.'s inner city, with a fantastic, growing, ongoing harvest of souls. God carried out His plan to perfection, and in an eight- to thirteen-week period, more than fifty thousand decisions for Christ were recorded through all the "Hope for L.A." activities. "Operation STITCHES" is now working in thirty-five different cities around the country.

The local ministry Paula and our group had teamed up with in Los Angeles had a strong television ministry, so we instantly gained national and international recognition for our involvement with the outreach. People began to fly in from all over the country and from around the world to help on the streets. Literally thousands of calls and letters came in, asking for help and training on how to reach the inner cities.

Out of this was born still another ministry for Without Walls, the International Training Center. Since its beginning in May 1994, the center has conducted special seminars and training programs three or four times a year for people of all ages, races, and denominations who really want to be equipped to do God's work. Because many individuals and small churches don't have the finances to pay training fees, the service is provided at no charge. In fact, we even house those who have no place to stay during the training.

187

Without Walls

Within the first two years, this new ministry helped prepare more than five thousand people to take the principles of Operation Explosion and other Without Walls inner-city evangelistic outreaches back to their home churches and cities, in states and countries around the globe. What are the results? It would take another book to report all that we've heard so far.

One church wrote back to say, "When we came to the Operation Explosion Seminar in February, we were averaging three hundred twenty-five people on Sunday morning. When we returned, we prepared our people for a month of evangelism in April. We had two thousand at our Easter egg hunt, with some sixty-five people accepting Christ. We had more than two thousand attending a three-night drama, with one hundred forty-seven accepting Christ. The Sundays before and after Easter we had four hundred fifty in attendance—on Easter Sunday we had six hundred thirteen in the morning service."

A lady came up to us at a meeting, weeping and crying. She said, "Oh, Pastor White, thank you. My husband and I came to your Operation Explosion Seminar from upper New York state. We had been in the ministry for over twenty years, and the most we ever had in our church was between seventeen and thirty people. We came to your training center and learned how to get out and do the work of the Lord. Back home, we went out on the streets for the first time. As a result, we have seen nine hundred sixty-three people saved! Our church is now exploding with growth!"

Here's one last example. A pastor writes, "We want you to know that you and your staff have made a serious impression on our lives. We are different people today than we were two weeks ago. Thank you for your time, your patience, and your persistence in making sure we had all the tools necessary to go back home and take our city for Christ. We have put into motion our plans to get out into the street, and the people of our church have caught the vision and are willing to do whatever is necessary to see it fulfilled."

Imagine what could happen to this nation—to the world—if there was at least one "church without walls" operating in each city and town. Can it happen? Is it possible? Indeed, it is happening. Virtually every day we hear a new report of a church somewhere that is responding to the heart of God and going out to reach the hopeless and hurting, the lost and broken, the precious needy souls for whom Christ died.

Thank God for every worker in every church who is taking the power of the gospel outside the walls and reaching people at the point of their need.

"Just do it" is not
the key to success.
You must do it and keep
doing it!

Persistence

How long does it take to rescue and restore a troubled soul? How many times should you try to befriend and witness to someone who is lost and without God?

It took us a year to reach Becky. She was suspicious, hard, and bitter; she rebuffed every approach our visitation teams made in her neighborhood. She had lived in an inner-city housing project for thirteen years.

When we took Operation Explosion to her area each week, her children were excited about the clowns and the music, the laughter and fun, the snacks and goodies. And Becky agreed to let them attend as long as she personally didn't have to get involved.

Later we learned that Becky had married when she was only fifteen, and the marriage only lasted long enough to break her heart... and leave her with a baby. Back with her parents, she continued to search for love, constantly dating and partying.

Her second marriage was an even worse experience. Even though Becky and her new husband had a new baby, the family fell apart. This husband treated Becky's daughter badly—to the degree that the state welfare agency threatened to take away her children. When she forced her husband to leave, he took all the furniture with him.

The scars from those kind of hurts don't heal quickly. So Becky watched warily as the church ministry team loved and blessed her children. The workers were not pushy, and they were consistent and faithful to be there every week. At Christmas, we took presents to all the children in the project.

So when we asked if the kids could ride the bus to church, Becky said yes, but she wouldn't go. She refused a second invitation, a third...a fifth. Then the kids started pleading with her to go with them. "It's a real cool place, Mom, come on!" So she thought, *Maybe I'd better go check out the place.*

The next Sunday, Becky got dressed and ready to go. But the bus didn't come—it had broken down that day. When the visitation team showed up later in the week, Becky tore into them like a tiger. "Why should I get ready if you're not going to come?" They assured her that they'd be there the next Sunday.

Early Sunday morning when I got to the church, Vicki grabbed my arm the minute I got out of the car. "The bus driver for the southside project didn't show up," she said.

"What do you want me to do about it?"

"I need you to drive," she said. "We can't miss two Sundays in a row." So I climbed on the bus and took off.

As I picked up kids and parents around the project, I recognized Becky coming out to the bus with her children. Knowing how long our workers had been trying to reach her, I made a special effort to welcome her. "Becky, it's good to see you today." She told us later how shocked she was in the service when the preacher turned out to be the "bus driver." It made a lasting impression on her to see that the pastor was also a servant.

Soon Becky was attending church every week...every time it was possible to be there. And in one service, she responded to a salvation invitation. What a joy it was to pray with her and help her receive deliverance and freedom from a lifetime of suffering and hurt.

With the church's encouragement and support, Becky was able

to get a job and begin earning a regular income. After a while, she was able to get off welfare and state assistance. It was a day of celebration when she moved out of the public housing project where she'd spent thirteen years and moved to her own apartment.

Becky was eager to begin ministering to other women and their children who were in the same predicament she'd been in. She became a fireball evangelist, tireless and intense. On one occasion, after she'd spoken about the work of the church in the inner cities before a group of ministries, she expressed concern to me about her lack of education. I said, "Becky, don't ever let anybody intimidate you about that. You may not have gone to college, but you have been well educated in life's school of hard knocks."

Becky spent about three and a half years working with Vicki as her assistant in Operation Explosion. During that time, she gained much knowledge and confidence and learned how to be an effective and efficient manager.

She is now the outreach director for a church in the northern state where her parents live, and she is duplicating many of Without Wall's outreaches and programs there. God continues to prosper her so that her family has bought their first home, and she has a new car to drive.

Is this kind of story worth an entire year of effort and ministry? Absolutely!

Be a participant, not
just a spectator.

The Student
Teaches the Teacher

A friend invited Jolene to visit Without Walls "just one time." She came...and never left. She loved the joyful atmosphere, the praise and worship, and the focus on practical, "get-the-job-done" faith. Jolene had attended church off and on for years, but she was amazed at the literally hundreds of ministries this church directed toward meeting people's needs.

Jolene had a special need. Although she was raising a family and working to help support them, she didn't have a high school education. She had dropped out of school in the tenth grade and never gone back. Many times over the years, she'd wished she had a diploma, often feeling inadequate and deprived because of the many basic things she'd never had a chance to learn.

Imagine her surprise to discover that Without Walls offered a state-approved GED (General Education Development) study program for people like her. The classes even fit in with her work schedule. So Jolene went back to school! There were about thirteen in the class, and together they learned English, math, science, history, social studies—all the core subjects.

Without Walls

It was a challenge to learn how to learn all over again. And it took special effort to find the time and energy to read and study after an already full day of working and taking care of her family. But Jolene was faithful. And after six months of concentrated effort, she took the state-administered test. She passed and was awarded the precious prize of her GED certificate.

She was very proud of her achievement. And what a great feeling of satisfaction she had the next time she filled out a job application and was able to check *yes* to the question about having earned a high school diploma or GED.

This outreach has proved to have a tremendous impact on entire families. When one member reaches this educational milestone, the whole family shares the pride and joy. When Miss Bonnie got her GED, our whole congregation celebrated. The oldest of four generations from one family at Without Walls, Miss Bonnie went back to school and got her GED when she was eighty-five!

Not only is this program beneficial to church members, it is also a great community service and a way to bring a relationship with unchurched people. There is a saying that goes like this: "Give a man a fish, and he'll eat for a day. Teach a man to fish, and he'll have food for a lifetime." We feel that our GED outreach helps "teach a man to fish." And in our case, the GED outreach is sponsored by the state, with government funding. What a deal!

But back to Jolene's story. "I know God had it all planned out for me to study for my GED at this church," she said. "Not only was it for my benefit, but for Miss Ginger, our teacher. She was not a regular at Without Walls, and God had been dealing with her. Several times when we students would be talking about the Lord, I noticed that she was teary-eyed.

"Then one night Miss Ginger was really shaken up by the Lord—broken and crying. 'I don't know what's wrong with me,' she said. 'This has never happened to me before.'

"'Well, Miss Ginger,' I said, 'you need to give your heart to the Lord. Do you want to do that?' She nodded through her tears, and we knelt right there in the classroom, and she prayed and gave her heart to the Lord. What a thrill! That was the best part of the whole GED program.

"Not only was my life enriched by completing my high school education and getting a GED certificate, but also the Lord used me to minister to someone and lead her to Jesus. It's an awesome feeling. Now I look for opportunities to share Jesus with others. I'll never be the same again."

There are people who
are called to you and
people who are called
through you.

The Most Important Work I've Ever Done

He walks like a cat...gracefully, silently, purposefully, and unhurried. Without trying, his movements make you aware of his tremendous physical power and spiritual strength.

Shawn holds a seventh-degree black belt in five different martial arts styles, is a world kick-boxing champion, and is a member of the Martial Arts Hall of Fame. He is a professional stunt man who has performed his craft before the camera in several movies, including *Smokey and the Bandit II, SemiTough,* and *Miami Blues.* He is a professional dancer with many television production credits.

"I've been lots of places and done lots of things in my life," said Shawn. "Some things I'm not too proud of. I got involved in lots of stuff in the devil's world. I was a professional dancer in a nightclub for eighteen years, and I served as head of security. My work in movies, doing commercials, and making TV appearances exposed me to some people and lifestyles that weren't so good. I also operated a fitness center, teaching karate, boxing, and kick boxing, and being a personal trainer. But there was always something missing in my life. I didn't have a personal experience with Jesus Christ as my Lord and Savior.

"Now my life has been radically changed. All that was once important to me in the world is now behind me. God has given me a fresh, new chance to do something really important. When I walked onto the parking lot at Without Walls, something came over me. And when I met Pastor Randy and Pastor Paula and heard them minister, I knew those blue-eyed white folks had a direct line to God."

Now Shawn is a dedicated man of God. For years he had made appearances in schools, giving martial arts demonstrations and performing feats of strength. His message, although completely secular at that time, encouraged personal purity—no alcohol, tobacco, or drugs—and warned against involvement with gangs or troublemakers.

Now in his forties, Shawn has become an evangelist, sharing his testimony of how God can give life real meaning and purpose. He continues to minister to youth as a member of Without Walls' outreach team, Conquering Force. This group features several physical fitness champions, all of whom perform strongman feats like breaking chains, chopping stacks of bricks with their bare hands, bending iron bars, blowing up hot water bottles, and tearing phone directories in half. But the real purpose of each performance is to include a powerful witness for the Lord Jesus Christ.

After one of his first ministry trips with Conquering Force, Shawn was excited and "pumped" at the response. "We had souls saved, man—young souls! Sharing my testimony and then seeing those kids praying and receiving Christ—what an incredible thrill! I can't wait for the next trip.

"I'm grateful for this opportunity. When Pastor Michael, director of Conquering Force, invited me to join the team, I was elated. I want to do as much as I can for God. This is the most important work I've ever done!"

Lay down whatever
is separating you
from God.

Breaking the Curse

"Pastor, I have something to tell you—I'm pregnant!" The young woman sitting across the desk from me was not married. Her name was Julie, and she'd been an active member of our church for about a year, then she dropped out of sight for two or three months. As far as I knew, her parents weren't Christians—at least, they didn't actively attend any church.

Coming back to church in her situation took a lot of courage, I knew. She obviously was nervous and didn't know what to expect from me. "I'm so glad you came to see me, Julie. We've missed you and are so glad to have you back. Are you okay?"

Heaving a sigh of relief, Julie nodded and dabbed at her brimming eyes.

"Do you want to tell me what happened?" She did.

When Julie gave her life to Christ, she experienced a great spiritual high and became an exuberant and enthusiastic believer. After a time, she even enrolled in our Master Pastor Internship Program, learning how the church functions and receiving training in evangelism and personal ministry. She was a great student, faithful in carrying out all her assignments.

Unbeknownst to anyone at the church, Julie was vulnerable in two critical areas of her life. First, at conversion she felt that the lure and temptation of sin was over. She told herself that she refused to ever make her former mistakes again or repeat the behavior she'd been ashamed of in the past. Second, she didn't understand the importance of seeking godly counsel and keeping company with people of faith who are strong in Christ.

When a man started coming on to her, she soon found herself succumbing to the very temptations she had sworn would never overpower her again. And instead of running to her friends for support and help, she dropped out of church altogether and tried to handle the situation on her own. Two months later she was pregnant ... and alone.

Telling her parents wasn't a major trauma because premarital pregnancy was a common pattern in her family. It seemed to crop up in every generation. So although they had expected more from Julie and were a bit disappointed, they weren't too shocked.

Going back to church was a little more unsettling. Julie didn't know how she would be received. She expected to encounter disapproval, maybe even rejection from some. She told a girlfriend, "It's just a natural reaction for people to criticize. But that's okay, I'll just have to deal with it."

To her amazement, there was no negative reaction from anybody. After leading her in a prayer of rededication to Christ in my office, I suggested that she should resume her training for ministry by attending my Timothy classes Sunday morning and evening. These are mentoring sessions in which I share my vision and my heart, including specific, practical ways to be effective in various situations.

"Do you mean it, Pastor?" she asked. "Is it really okay for me to come?"

"You bet it is," I said. "Welcome back, and I'll see you Sunday."

Every staff member met Julie with open arms and words of encouragement. A few months later, someone in the church gave her a baby shower, which was well attended. Paula made it a point to be there with a gift. Her card said, "Julie, I love you. Here's a gift for your baby."

When Julie's baby girl was born, she had everything she needed, from clothing to crib. And at church, that child has lots of uncles and aunts and grandparents to hold her and love on her.

Several days a week, Julie brings the baby with her to church where she is a volunteer in the Operation Explosion outreach office. "I have so much more compassion for other people now," said Julie. "When I see individuals struggling and having problems, I know they don't need condemnation or criticism. I can say to them, 'I understand where you're coming from. I've been there. And there is hope and help for you.'

"I like to have my little girl in this environment," said Julie. "I don't want her exposed to the things I grew up with. I want to keep her surrounded by godly people who will help her learn what's right and good. With God's help, my baby will break that generational curse and the cycle of sin."

Inasmuch as ye have
done it unto one
of the least of these
my brethren, ye have
done it unto me.
　　—Jesus, Matthew 25:40

Fire!

Peter woke with a start, hearing a crackling and popping sound. The clock said it was almost two o'clock in the morning, but there were bright light and intense heat coming in the windows. Suddenly he heard his mother shout, "Fire!" Then he smelled smoke, and he was wide awake.

Peter called 911 to report the fire, then he ran to help his mother out of the house. Once she was safe, he went back in to awaken his eighty-seven-year-old father and help him out.

By then the fire was raging in the house and the one next door, which his parents had rented out to three Mexican boys. Two of them made it out, one with second degree burns on his arms and back. The third boy was overcome by smoke and didn't make it out. Although the firefighters arrived quickly, the intensity of the flames kept them from going in for the other boy. By the time the fire was brought under control and they got to him, he was dead.

Peter had only been in Tampa a short time, but he had been attending church at Without Walls. That morning he had planned to go horseback riding with some friends, Jack and Kathy, who also attended the church, so he called to let them know he couldn't make it because there'd been "a little fire."

Within the hour, Jack and Kathy were there to see if they could help. They were astounded at the devastation. Both houses were totally destroyed. Peter was rummaging through the debris of his mother's burned-out bedroom, looking for her pocketbook and wallet. He was in his boxer shorts—everything else he owned in the world had burned.

Jack and Kathy pitched in to help, offering encouragement and support. They gave Peter some clothes and helped him get his parents into temporary quarters.

They also helped minister to the Mexican boys from the burned-out house next door. They were almost in shock from the death of their friend and the loss of all their possessions. The young man who had been burned was in pain. He had been taken to two different hospitals but had gotten only minimal treatment—a gauze bandage and a prescription.

Jack phoned the church for help and, within hours, various outreaches of Without Walls were mobilized. The burn victim was treated by Dr. Bethany Combs at our own Operation Med-Care; his burns were carefully cleaned and covered with antibiotic ointment, then wrapped with protective bandages, and proper pain medication was dispensed.

Peter and the two Mexican boys were brought to a service. The news of the fire had spread, and they were met with an outpouring of love and compassionate attention. I asked the church to gather around them and pray. I said, "Here is one of our own who is in need. Let's pray for him, his parents, and his neighbors here." Then I called for our Spanish-speaking members to come minister to the Mexican boys. Both of them were very appreciative and responsive, and they received Jesus Christ as their Lord and Savior. Right in the middle of a service, we stopped and spent twenty minutes or more blessing these young men.

Later we were able to place the boys with Island Breeze, an area ministry affiliated with Youth With A Mission that was able to provide temporary housing, Spanish-speaking counselors, and assistance in getting them back on their feet. A nurse who attended

Without Walls volunteered to drive from her home in St. Petersburg to Tampa to change the bandages of the burn victim every day.

Some might question why we'd invest so much in people who would probably never attend our church, never be able to serve or help us, never contribute a dime. Besides, it would have been easier to just refer them somewhere else because of the language barrier. But the answer is simple—Jesus said to do it. In Matthew 25, He said, "I was a stranger, and ye took me in." When? "Inasmuch as ye have done it unto one of the least of these my brethren, ye have done it unto me" (Matt. 25:35, 40).

The Without Walls congregation also gave a generous special offering to help Peter and his parents get into another house. Various individuals began donating clothing, furniture, dishes, silverware—everything to help set up housekeeping again. Before it was over, Peter and his parents had scores of new friends, and our members had rallied once again to find practical expressions for their faith.

This is the Good Samaritan Christianity Jesus talked about. This is what it means to have a church that operates—not just for an hour on Sunday morning—but every day, outside the walls of the sanctuary, out where hurting people are struggling with the problems and needs of life.

Just because
they aren't perfect
doesn't mean
they're not welcome.

The Power Pig

There is a pop radio station in Tampa called "The Power Pig." The on-air personalities are loud, brash, and irreverent, constantly making explicit, graphic comments in an attempt to be "hip" and shocking. They play the most current "hip-hop" music, often with very worldly, suggestive lyrics. Naturally, they have a huge listening audience.

One day someone from the station called the church and asked us to send someone they could interview about the work we were doing with the needy and homeless. We sent Pat, who was pastor of our ministry to the homeless, down to the station. He took along an article about the church that had recently appeared in *Charisma* magazine.

The interview went terrific. Pat answered questions about what the church was doing to help the poor, sharing example after example of individuals who had been able to get out of the alleys and gutters and back into a stable, productive life with God's help. The deejay doing the interview got more and more interested and excited.

When Pat asked if he could read some excerpts from the magazine article, which referred to us as the "vegetable-soup church," the deejay took it and began to read it aloud over the air. As he read, the power of the Holy Spirit began to move in that super-secular radio station, and the deejay began to get choked up. He read most of the article, fighting back tears, stopping often to clear his throat.

Finally he put down the article and made a personal appeal. "Listen to me—anyone depressed, on drugs, or with a need, get on the phone or get down to that church right away!"

Pat invited the deejay to attend a special benefit program for the homeless at our church, and he agreed to come. I had them put him right on the front row. I wanted him to get under the anointing of the Holy Spirit and feel the convicting power of God. Afterward he came to me and said, "I'm really touched by what you're doing for needy people, Pastor. I've never been in a church service before, but I enjoyed every minute of it!"

What was the attraction? First, he had seen the practical, loving side of our Christianity in our outreach to the homeless. He saw Christians making a difference in their community. Then he came and experienced for himself what it means to be in touch with heaven.

About this time, Michael, our youth pastor, planned a "Rock da House" party. He got permission to pass out flyers on both junior high and high school campuses. He organized Christian dance and rap contests, and he arranged for this awesome deejay to play the music. They moved everything out of the sanctuary and put up professional lighting and sound systems.

More than eight hundred young people attended the concert, many as a result of the "Power Pig" deejay's on-air appeal. At first the kids could not believe they were really in a church because, as they put it, "It's so cool!" And once the music and activities began, they liked being in such a fun environment that wasn't charged with smutty, suggestive song lyrics and worldly remarks by the deejay.

At the end of the evening, our youth pastor ministered the Word, sharing briefly his personal experiences with drugs and prison, and his testimony of deliverance and restoration. Many of the teens came forward for prayer and came to know Christ as their Savior that night.

The people from the congregation who volunteered to help sponsor and chaperone this event were amazed and impressed that eight hundred kids could have such a good time with no drinking, no drugs, and no trouble.

The concert was such a success that we did a couple more, which also went well. The only problem was the many hours of work and the wear and tear of setting up and tearing down all the equipment to get the sanctuary ready to use for church again. It was obvious that this kind of activity needed its own permanent space. So we discontinued the "Rock da House" events for a while. But the idea that was birthed then became the prototype for our present Club X teen club, which operates each weekend from its home in our four-story office and activities building.

To reap a different
harvest, you must plant
different seed.

All I Know Is That He Loves Me

Cindy is looking forward to going to heaven someday—she's already spent too much time in hell.

Her mother was a drug-addicted stripper who abandoned Cindy and her sister when they were two and three years old. Cindy's father supported his daughters, but by the time they were ten and eleven, he left them on their own in a house far back in the woods.

Cindy's sister kept running away from home just so she could be around people. So Cindy was alone, hungry, and afraid all through her growing-up years. Why didn't anybody want to be around her? Sometimes she'd walk to friends' houses—boys and girls—and climb in their bedroom windows so their parents wouldn't know she was spending the night. She also remembers sleeping out in the doghouse several nights just to be near something that was alive. And to this day, she doesn't like the dark.

She had a boyfriend, but he didn't want the responsibility of supporting her. So at age fourteen, a relative introduced her to a pimp who put her to work "dancing" in all-nude strip clubs. Strangely enough, she sort of liked getting all the attention and having the spotlight shining on her. And she earned enough money to buy nice clothes, cigarettes, beer, and all she wanted to eat.

She and her boyfriend got along better while she was bringing in some cash. Before long she was pregnant. When she started showing, she couldn't strip. No work, no pay, and she ended up on welfare until her son was born. When she regained her figure, she went back to the strip clubs.

Cindy was popular with the customers because of her imaginative and energetic dance programs, starting with a slow, slinky, sensuous pace and building to a frenzy of wild, uninhibited, totally abandoned debauchery. Her performances also attracted the attention of photographers for *Playboy* magazine, and she did several photo shoots modeling sexy lingerie, skimpy bikinis, and less.

The attention and "success" went to Cindy's head. From feeling she was a "nobody," she became conceited, self-centered, and a braggadocio. She felt she must be very beautiful and talented to attract so much attention and be in such demand in the clubs.

In disgust, her boyfriend decided to visit another state for a week, taking their son with him. Cindy was elated at the prospect of having a whole week with no responsibility so she could do what she wanted. She and a girlfriend planned to live it up and go out every night.

The first night they went to a club, dressed in what she felt were "classy, sexy" clothes that showed enough to attract lots of attention. She was pumped up, egotistical, and acting tough and "bad." Cindy remembers slipping past a man with no legs whose wheelchair was partially blocking the aisle. "Watch his feet, Angie," she mockingly warned her friend, and then she laughed boisterously.

After leaving the club, they went to the girlfriend's house, where Cindy was persuaded to try taking a pill. "What is it?" she asked.

"Oh, it will make you feel good. It's called Ecstasy, and everybody's doing it right now. Come on, try it."

So Cindy took half of the pill, but she didn't notice that it had any affect at all. Then on the way to her own apartment with her friend, she took the other half. Within minutes, the drug, which elevates sensual arousal and tends to enhance the sense of touch, hit her hard. She began screaming in excitement, ripping off her clothes and clawing the top liner of her car with her long finger-nails. "Oh, this feels so good," she cried. "I love this drug. I don't ever want to come down."

At Cindy's third-floor apartment, she and her girlfriend ended up in the bathtub together, rubbing shampoo and lotion on each other's bodies, getting more and more drawn into sexual stimula-tion. She'd never been involved with any gay or bisexual activity before, and even in her drug-driven state, Cindy was aware that the situation was getting way out of hand. She tried to stand up, but she slipped and fell, slamming her head hard against the bathtub.

Although hurt and stunned by the fall, Cindy managed to crawl into the living room. Wet and naked, rocking back and forth on her knees, she tried to pray. "I know this is wrong, God," she gasped. "Forgive me for all my sins. But please don't let me die like this. I don't want my little boy to know I died on drugs."

At that moment, she was aware of a "presence" near her. It seemed so real she could envision seeing a figure standing before her, which she thought must be Jesus. And she heard a voice saying, "I love you, baby." Cindy recalls feeling that the love she had never had in all of her life suddenly flooded into her being, filled her whole heart, mind, and body.

"It was incredible—I'd never felt anything like that before," said Cindy. "But the feeling quickly passed, and then I was overcome with an overwhelming remorse and regret for my past lifestyle and bad attitudes. I guess I went into total hysteria and began trying to punish myself for my sins. I bashed my head against the wall, dug my long fingernails into my eyes and face, then tried holding my breath until I passed out.

"When that was unsuccessful, I hurled myself against the window. Then I dragged the vacuum cleaner out of the closet and smashed the glass. Without one thought, I hurled myself out of the third-story window."

Cindy woke up in the hospital, still suffering the aftermath of the drug she had taken. Then she noticed she couldn't feel her feet or legs, and she recalled her callous remark about the man in the wheelchair. She became so agitated and upset that she had to be sedated again.

Without Walls

The nurse who took care of Cindy was a member of Without Walls International Church. In addition to being a skilled medical professional, Jeannie was also spiritually perceptive. She recognized that much of her patient's pain and distress was spiritual, not medical. So she began inviting friends from the church to visit Cindy and sending people from our pastoral staff in to talk with her. Several times, someone prayed with Cindy in the hospital, and her name was added to our prayer list at church.

After recovering from what, remarkably, were fairly minor injuries, Cindy went home. But her life was dramatically changed. She got out of her boyfriend's bed and stopped the strip dancing. This meant she had to learn how to trust God for her finances.

"It's pretty hard sometimes," she said, "but now I'm letting God take charge of my life. I'm still facing some big challenges, but the Lord's still working on me. Can you believe that He loves me enough to change me? My nurse friend, Jeannie, still keeps in touch. She's helped me find some wonderful friends at Without Walls. I'm becoming a different person.

"I can't explain all that has happened. When I was doing my worst, God did His best for me. That's pretty awesome. All I know is that He loves me!"

The dog may bark,
but the train keeps
on rolling.

The God
of the Valleys

First Kings 20 recounts one of the most amazing dramas in all of the Bible. The stage is filled with mighty armies, multiplied thousands of fighting men. Benhadad, king of Syria, is on the march with his hosts, along with the armies of thirty-two other kings, with troops, horsemen, and chariots. They have besieged Samaria and sent a message to Ahab, king of Israel.

In boastful arrogance, Benhadad demands all of Israel's silver and gold, as well as Ahab's wives and children. "I'll take the best for myself," he said. Then when Ahab tried not to provoke him, the cruel Syrian monarch raised the ante. "I've changed my mind. I'll send my servants to go through your palace, and anything they see that they think you treasure, they'll seize and bring to me."

Ahab counseled with the elders of Israel who said, "Don't consent to this. We'll take our chances on the battlefield."

Benhadad and the other thirty-two kings had been sitting around drinking, and when he heard Ahab's response to his demands, he was furious. He immediately ordered his troops to array themselves for battle. But he and the kings kept on drinking.

Without Walls

When Israel's small army marched out of Samaria to defend their nation, Benhadad derisively ordered his troops to go and capture all of Israel's soldiers alive. But when they went out against Israel, they were defeated. A great battle began, which turned into a rout, then a slaughter. King Benhadad himself barely managed to escape by riding with the horsemen as they ran away.

For the next year, Benhadad sat around licking his wounds, angry and humiliated by his terrible defeat. Finally he was able to regroup and reorganize his army to go out to battle again. His advisers said, "The reason the Israelites were able to prevail is because their gods are gods of the hills. But if you will fight them in the plains, surely we shall be stronger than them."

Bad advice! But Benhadad listened to it and started marching toward Israel again. God had already warned Ahab what was going to happen, so he was prepared. The prophet of God said, "Because the Syrians have said that the Lord is only the God of the hills, but not the valleys, therefore I will deliver all this great multitude into your hand."

Now, Syria outnumbered Israel ten to one. And they were massing their great forces on the plains and in the valleys, planning to annihilate Israel's forces in retaliation for the great defeat they had suffered the year before. But they were doomed.

When the battle began, the outnumbered soldiers of Israel began a fierce hand-to-hand attack, and the Syrians fell before them like animals in a slaughterhouse. A hundred thousand Syrian foot soldiers died in a single day. Of those that retreated into the city of Aphek, twenty-seven thousand more died when a wall collapsed and fell on them.

The God we serve is victorious on the mountaintop and also in the valley. Everybody likes the mountaintop experiences. They love to sing and shout, to enjoy the praise and worship, to wave the banner of victory. But you can't live on the mountaintop. The air is thin and cold up there, and after a while you get dizzy and lightheaded up on the mountain. I want you to know that God's power is good on Sunday morning when you're singing "Going Up to the High Places," but it's also good on Monday morning when you're surrounded by people cursing and telling dirty jokes and blowing smoke in your face. God is God of the mountain, and He is also God of the valley.

I've enjoyed some great times of success in my ministry. God has been so good to me. I've felt the precious anointing of the Holy Spirit upon me and God's power surging through my being. I've preached to thousands in great auditoriums across America. I've watched people come out of their wheelchairs, healed instantaneously by the power of the living God. I've seen blind eyes opened and made whole. I've preached in the upper room in Jerusalem and witnessed a mighty demonstration of the Holy Ghost. I know what it is like to be on the mountaintop.

But the greatest joy I've ever experienced is not up there...but when I was in the valley. That's when the Holy Spirit would come in and breathe His breath of life into me. He would wrap His arms of love and mercy and compassion around me and say, "I am your God—the God of the valley."

For you who are in the valley right now, let me give you some spiritual prescriptions. The Word says, "For this purpose the Son of God was manifested, that he might destroy the works of the devil" (1 John 3:8). The Word says, "No weapon that is formed against thee shall prosper" (Isa. 54:17). The Word says, "When the enemy shall come in like a flood, the spirit of the LORD shall lift up a standard against him" (Isa. 59:19).

The Word says, "Who shall separate us from the love of Christ? Shall tribulation, or distress, or persecution, or famine, or nakedness, or peril, or sword?...Nay, in all these things we are more than conquerors through him that loved us. For I am persuaded, that neither death, nor life, nor angels, nor principalities, nor powers, nor things present, nor things to come, nor height, nor depth, nor any other creature, shall be able to separate us from the love of God, which is in Christ Jesus our Lord" (Rom. 8:35, 37–39).

Are you getting it? No creature, no devil, no demon in hell can destroy us! What does the Word say? "Submit yourselves therefore to God. Resist the devil, and he will flee from you" (James 4:7). What does the Word say? "Greater is he that is in you, than he that is in the world" (1 John 4:4).

God is for you. He is with you. He is your shield and protector, and the lifter up of your head. He rejoices with you on the mountaintop. In the valley, He restores your soul. He is with you when you go out and when you come in. God is faithful. "Jesus Christ the same yesterday, and to day, and for ever" (Heb. 13:8).

That is why you are well able to go out and help take your city for Christ. You have an experience with God, and you have put it to the test. You can be a witness. No, you don't have to be a theologian, have dozens of scripture verses memorized, or be trained in psychological counseling. All you have to do is say, "This is what happened to me. When I was lost, He found me. When I was down, He lifted me up. And He'll do the same for you." That's all there is to it. Someone once said that witnessing is just one beggar telling another where to find bread. You can do that. Just brag on Jesus—He'll do the rest. He said, "I, if I be lifted up from the earth, will draw all men unto me" (John 12:32).

You can make a difference in your community. You can be a soul-winner. You can be the salt of the earth and the light of the world. God will help you reach your family, your neighbors, and your loved ones. He loves them even more than you do.

Will you do it? Will you help take your city for Christ? I promise you that God will answer your heart's cry when you pray.

If not me, then who? If not now, when? If not here, where?

The Need Is the Call

S ometimes people say to me, "What you do is wonderful. It's obvious that you have a real call of God upon your life to help poor and needy people. But I'm not sure if I'm called to do that."

The truth is that you don't need a call from God to do this work. The need is the call! When you see a person in need and you take care of that need, you are answering the call. When you meet people at the point of their need, you have the precious opportunity to lead them to the Lord.

There's nothing confusing or difficult about the call of God. The simple basics of Practical Christianity 101 are to reach out in love to the homeless, the inner-city children, the divorcee, the prisoner, the prostitute, the homosexual—in short, the so-called undesirables of our world. The "blessed" Jesus talked about in Matthew 25 are those who, when they saw the hungry, they gave them meat; when they saw the thirsty, they gave them drink; when they saw the stranger, they took him in. The "blessed" saw the naked and clothed them, they saw the sick and imprisoned and visited them (see vv. 34-36).

Without Walls

The broken and wounded make up a very large portion of the people of this world. They are the End-Time harvest.

Where are the laborers for the harvest? Why hasn't God "called" more fishers of men? I believe He has, but too many haven't answered. Instead of saying, "Here am I, Lord; send me," we've tried to put God on hold until we're not so busy...or until we feel better prepared.

Let me tell you, people have needs at the most inconvenient times. Opportunities to witness and help usually come when your schedule is full and you're at your busiest.

Not long ago I stopped off to get my hair cut. I'd planned to use the time I was in the barber chair looking at my appointment book for the week and thinking and praying about some decisions I had to make. But God changed my plans. The lady who was supposed to cut my hair was not available, so another woman named Amber took over. As I spoke with her for a moment, I could immediately tell that she had some desperate needs in her life.

Amber was a "prodigal daughter," running from God. Her three brothers were all preachers, but at age thirty-one, her life was in shambles. She was a part-time striptease dancer, abusing cocaine. Her boyfriend, who was in the shop that day, was addicted to gambling. They were in desperate circumstances, searching for something to salvage their lives. Now, I didn't have to be a trained spiritual counselor to learn these things. I found out all of this just by starting a conversation, then listening.

In a few minutes, I looked at Amber through the mirror above the counter and said, "Can I pray with you right now?" I didn't have to quote several scriptures or give a theological explanation of the plan of salvation. Desperate people are like a crop that is ready for harvesting.

Right there in the middle of that hair salon, Amber and I prayed. Everyone around us quieted down and listened. Amber asked me to pray that she would have peace inside, and as I did, she received the Prince of Peace, the Lord Jesus Christ.

When I left, she was smiling through her tears. "I feel so good inside," she said. "Thank God He found me."

Was it anything I had done? Not at all. She wanted to be found.

She just needed someone to listen, to care, and to point her in the right direction. And in just a few minutes, she ran from a life without peace, without hope, and without direction—straight into the arms of God.

Our Lord is not only able, but willing and eager to restore the broken and wounded people of this world. As God's Word says, "Where sin abounded, grace did much more abound" (Rom. 5:20).

Are you called? That's the wrong question. Instead, ask—Are there people around you who are broken, lonely, hurt, and crying out for something to fill the void in their lives? Their need is your call. Look! Listen! Do you see them? Can you hear them? That "something" they are seeking is the message of restoration. And you are the messenger.

This is your mission—the people you meet at your workplace, in your neighborhood, in a restaurant, at the barber shop. Are you getting the picture? Let that become your vision. You must have a vision—it's a matter of life or death. The Bible says plainly, "Where there is no vision, the people perish" (Prov. 29:18).

If what you have won't meet your need, it's not your harvest— it's your seed. You can never "outgive" God.

Treasures
of the Heart

In 1997 I invited Dr. Myles Munroe to come to Tampa for three days of special services in our church. Our people were hungry for a deeper move of God, and this dear brother ministered under a heavy anointing of the Holy Spirit. From the first service I could sense that something very special was about to happen.

On the second night, Dr. Munroe preached on "Treasures of the Heart," from a text in Matthew 6. Jesus said, "Lay not up for yourselves treasures upon earth, where moth and rust doth corrupt, and where thieves break through and steal: But lay up for yourselves treasures in heaven, where neither moth nor rust doth corrupt, and where thieves do not break through nor steal: For where your treasure is, there will your heart be also" (vv. 19-21).

When he finished speaking, people spontaneously began going to the altar, tears streaming down their faces. They began putting money, jewelry, rings, watches, and other items on the altar. Some wrote little notes saying they were giving a car, motorcycle, boat, even houses. Some of the items were very valuable—others had special sentimental value to the giver. In some cases, the item was not particularly expensive, but like the widow's mites in the Bible, it represented all the person had to give.

I was totally overwhelmed by this great outpouring. I was so touched that the tears wouldn't stop flowing; the lump in my throat nearly choked me. "I can't receive these things, Lord," I whispered. "They are too precious!"

And the voice of God spoke back, deep within me. "They are not giving these things to you, but for Me and My work. Don't hinder or interfere with what I am doing in the people's lives!"

As I watched the people putting their most precious possessions on the altar, I could only stand weeping until I had no more tears. I knew what these offerings cost these dear folks. They were giving their all.

In the days that followed, people kept bringing all kinds of things to the church. They brought coin collections, baseball cards, heirloom dishes, bikes, stereos, watches, wedding rings, fur coats, title deeds to property—someone even gave the church a medical center! Not one of the donors asked for acknowledgment or recognition. They were giving because they wanted to see the vision of the church come to pass—they wanted to make a difference.

We had not scheduled the special meeting in the hope of financial gain, although the church was facing great needs every single week to finance our ministries and outreaches to the homeless and poor who could give us nothing in return. I had not even mentioned our ongoing financial challenge to Dr. Munroe. His message on "Treasures of the Heart" had to be prompted by the Holy Spirit.

Before he left, Dr. Munroe said to me, "You don't know it yet, but something has broken in the spiritual realm within your people. You will see an 'Ebenezer' in your life—a place where you no longer do the battle, but God fights for you as He did for the Israelites in 1 Samuel 7:10–12. I believe the Lord is saying, 'The people have been put to the test, so now they can be trusted with mammon, or material things. Since they have given Me their treasures, now I am going to trust them with My treasures and My anointing.'"

The next Sunday, the anointing of God was so strong in our services that the people sat in awe in His presence. In the evening service, I was almost afraid to even move to get someone to turn the lights on in the tent as it got dark. Everyone realized that God was working and moving in our midst.

The amount of money given during the meeting was more than we normally would have received in several weeks. It was just enough to help us get current on our budget—and it came just in time. Paula and I and our ministerial staff realized that it had to be a miracle of God's provision.

As it turned out, it was just the beginning of a chain of miraculous events.

That same week, I got an urgent call from a man who operated several missionary television stations around the world who was facing an emergency need. "I've asked several churches to help, but no one has come through. And time is running out."

He said that the transmitter at their station in West Africa had broken down and had to be replaced at a cost of thirty thousand dollars. If they didn't get a new transmitter and resume broadcasting within three months, their license would be revoked. Once it was revoked, it would be given to someone else, and they'd never get it back.

I knew this man and his ministry to be genuine and trustworthy. So I had no doubts that his story was true and that this was a valid need. But after the tremendous outpouring we'd just received from the people of our church, how could I go to them and ask them to give to another project? *If I ask them to give to this,* I thought, *they will lynch me!*

Without Walls is not a wealthy church by any means. We have lots of ordinary, hardworking people and many, many who are poor and struggling to make ends meet, still in the process of being restored from the dire straits of poverty. We don't have large numbers of wealthy members.

I was well aware that these people already were helping support multiplied scores of ministries that were reaching into the community, feeding the poor, clothing the naked, reaching the homeless. We were doing a major building renovation, opening a school and a Bible college, and meeting various other obligations.

As all these things were running through my mind as valid reasons why we could not help with the television transmitter project the man said, "This station in West Africa broadcasts the gospel to more than two million souls!"

Two million souls! "I'll do it!" I shouted on the phone. "Souls are why we exist, what I breathe, sleep, eat, and live for. Reaching souls is our purpose as a church and my call as a minister."

The next Sunday, I got up before my people and presented the need to them. I was almost afraid to look them in the eye. I told them I proposed to give a tithe of our church income until the transmitter was paid for. No one lynched me. There wasn't even one complaint. And the amount of our tithes and offerings that Sunday went up!

The very next morning, I was in the office at 8:30. I was writing out the check for our tithe toward the transmitter. The ink was not even dry on the check when my secretary came rushing into my office, excitedly insisting that there was a call I needed to take right away.

The lady on the phone said, "Pastor White, you don't know me. I don't attend your church. But I know what you have been doing in the inner city, and I've just heard about the transmitter for West Africa you are trying to buy. Would you mind if I bless the church with the thirty thousand dollars for the transmitter?"

Would I mind? I almost burst out laughing for joy. The lady and her husband came to my office later that morning and gave me a cashier's check for thirty thousand dollars.

Before they left my office, they asked me to tell them about our church and any needs we might have. I briefly shared with them the concept of a church without walls and our vision to reach our city for Jesus. When I finished, the husband took a deep breath and said, "Pastor, I feel we need to do something to help in what you are doing. I want to give you one hundred thousand dollars."

Before I could say a word, the wife said, "Wait just a minute. We need to talk about this privately."

I excused myself and left them alone in my office. I didn't know what was going on. But within minutes they opened the door and asked me to come back in.

"We have come to a decision," said the husband. "Four years ago we were terribly in debt. It was so bad we could barely put food on the table. We told God if He would bless our business, we would give it back to help build His kingdom. Pastor, this is what we are going to do. Tomorrow we are going to bring in a cashier's check for half a million dollars."

And they did!

Since the people of Without Walls gave the "Treasures of the Heart" offerings, we can't keep up with the miracles of God's provision. Dozens of new ministry opportunities have opened up. On one particular day, nine major miraculous events took place.

Why has there been such supernatural provision and prosperity? I believe there are some definite reasons. First, we have been obedient to do what God has asked us to do. We are continually restoring broken lives and evangelizing our city. I have learned that if God can get it through you, then He can get it to you!

Secondly, as Solomon wrote, "He that hath pity upon the poor lendeth unto the LORD; and that which he hath given will he pay him again" (Prov. 19:17). I believe when you reach out to those less fortunate, God will reach out to you and supernaturally pour out His blessings.

Let go of what is in your hand, and God will let go of what is in His hand.

The Miracle Continues

Hurricanes and tents don't go together well. On more than one occasion, the inflated "super dome" structure that served as a sanctuary for Without Walls came out second-best in a meeting with a storm. The last time, it was completely leveled by a freak tornado—fortunately, not during a service.

Somehow, our maintenance team valiantly found a way to get it back in service. But all of us could see the handwriting on the plasticized wall. We had reached the point where we had to have a solid, substantial, permanent structure. Besides, we had outgrown the dome and were forced to have five services each weekend to accommodate the crowds.

We began looking around for a suitable existing structure that might meet our needs. The building we really wanted was a large soft drink factory and warehouse next door to our four-story office building, but we'd never been able to come to terms with the owner. A major shopping mall had been planned to go across the street from the soft drink company, making that property extremely valuable. We heard that two or three major hotels were bidding for the site.

After trying unsuccessfully to acquire another major property, we were back to square one. Trying not to let myself be disappointed, I prayed, "Lord, what are we going to do now?" I felt a sense of urgency to get something going, but at the same time I also felt strongly that God was at work in our behalf and everything was going to be all right.

A few days later I got a call from the soft drink company's representative. "Pastor," he asked, "are you still interested in this property?"

"Absolutely."

"Well, I want you to have it. You told us you wanted to buy it two years ago, and we know you need it. So although we could get more for it, we've decided to help you get it. We're coming down on the price almost a half million dollars, and we'll work with you however we can to make a deal that will work for you."

Talk about excited! Our advisors told us that if we acquired this property and connected it to our existing office campus, the value of both pieces would increase in value dramatically—to as much as twenty million dollars! And the existing factory/warehouse structure—one hundred thirty thousand square feet—was perfectly suited for our expansion needs.

From that one building, we could create a five-thousand-seat sanctuary with a production stage suitable for television, a large food storage and distribution center, a large kitchen and food serving area for feeding needy and homeless people, and a gymnasium for our youth activity center. With a bit of remodeling, the outside of the building would look very classy and nice.

But that's not all. We're developing a master plan that provides for a mini-mall complex to be developed between our office center and the new structure. This facility will have spaces for small workshops and retail stores to enable struggling families and single parents to start their own businesses and begin making their own way. In such an ideal location, who knows where such an enterprise could go.

But back to the story. Even at the reduced price, buying this new facility is our biggest step of faith ever. We had been planting seed for the substantial harvest we knew would be necessary for any real estate transaction. God had spoken to me to fly to Dallas and "sow" a gift of ten thousand dollars into Pastor T. D. Jakes' ministry. I knew he was doing a great job of ministering to indigent people, but I had no idea how the Lord would provide the funds we had to have to proceed.

Three days later I received an overnight parcel from a woman who is very interested and supportive of this ministry. She sent a check for the full down payment on the new property, along with a note that said, "We're going to make sure you get that building!"

And we did. We have closed on the property and are planning to start the renovation immediately. Oh, I don't know where all the funds will come from to finish paying for the new space or to remodel and develop the building—but God does. And in His way and on His timetable, it will be done. We are believing God that we will have the building paid off within a year. This will multiply our ministry and strengthen our outreaches to reach the city of Tampa for Christ.

I can hardly wait to see how He does it.

You can't clean a fish
until you catch it.

The Harvest Is Ugly

One day Jesus and His disciples were on the way from Judea to Galilee, when He said, "I need to go through Samaria." Now, this was not His original destination, and the village where He ended up may even have been a bit out of the way. Jesus was really saying, "I was on My way to do one thing, and I was arrested by the Holy Ghost to do something different."

When they got to Jacob's well, near the Samaritan village of Sychar, Jesus rested near the well while His disciples went to town to buy food. While He was there, a woman came to the well, and Jesus struck up a conversation with her. When she told Him she had no husband, Jesus shocked her by telling her the truth about herself. "Thou hast had five husbands; and he whom thou now hast is not thy husband" (John 4:18).

Why did Jesus have to go through Samaria? The woman at the well—the woman who had been married five times and was living with still another man—this worthless, sinful woman was a precious soul who was part of the Lord's harvest. He said, "My burden, My desire, My life's blood is to do the will of the Father who sent me." (See John 4:34.) "For the Son of man is come to seek and to save that which was lost" (Luke 19:10).

Many people would not even speak to this woman. She was a second-class citizen, a shameful hussy, living in sin. Everybody knew about her lifestyle and looked the other way when she passed by. After all, they had their religion, their rituals, and their traditions. It wasn't proper for them to have anything to do with her.

Before you get too harsh on the Samaritans, how do you think the church would treat her today? She might have to sit in the back if she visited some churches. Everybody would be whispering and gossiping about her. In some churches, the minister might even preach a sermon directly to her.

On the other hand, she might get ignored totally if she came. Nobody would pay any attention to her when she came in or went out. You see, so many in the Christian realm are so busy singing in the choir, playing a musical instrument, teaching a class, or being an usher that they've forgotten the real mission of the church. We've gotten so involved in operating the system that we've overlooked the reason for our existence.

THE CHURCH'S MISSION

Jesus said, "Lift up your eyes, and look on the fields; for they are white already to harvest" (John 4:35). Whatever else the church is doing is superfluous if we are not seeing the harvest beyond the four walls of the sanctuary.

We need to see beyond the carpeted aisles, stained-glass windows, and padded pews. We need to see beyond the board members and stewardship campaigns. Thank God for good church facilities, for church government, for plans and programs. But remember the harvest.

The church exists so we might save the lost and dying, feed the poor and needy. The church exists to reach a lost teenager, to help a family that is separated and divorced.

The harvest is out there, and it's not always pretty. Our families have been sheltered from the harvest. Our church work has distracted us from the harvest.

Randy White

CAN YOU SEE THE HARVEST?

The harvest is thirteen- and fourteen-year-old girls, pregnant, some for the second time...some of them from their own fathers. Incest is on an alarming increase—not in the deep, dark jungles of Africa, but right here in civilized, Christian America. It's ugly, and the churches don't want to see it. They turn their backs and say, "We don't know how to minister to that!"

The harvest is tens of thousands of people, middle-aged and older, the dropouts of society, sleeping on park benches, living in cardboard boxes under bridges. You'll find them, not just in New York and Los Angeles, but in virtually every town and city in the country. They languish and suffer and die while the church says, "Sing me another song, dance me another dance. Preach me happy and give me a Holy Ghost goose bump. Let me shout a little and go home saying, 'Man, that was a good service!'"

The church has been asleep for so long that it is still trying to minister to the perfect American family, with a mom and dad, a brother and a sister, a dog, and a white picket fence. Statistics now say that only seven out of a hundred families fit that description. Today's families have single parents, or stepparents, or couples with kids labeled yours, mine, and ours. In today's homes, both mom and dad work, and the latchkey kids come to an empty house after school to do who knows what.

Thank God for the perfect American families with two parents and children and white picket fences. God bless them. But the church has to be the church to the other 93 percent who make up today's lost and dying generation.

Another issue—somehow the church has to get rid of "stinkin' religious thinkin'" and find a way to reach the soaring numbers of unmarried couples who live together for the sake of convenience. The religious crowd demands that they first "make some changes" so they can qualify to come to church. But as I tell my congregation, "You've got to catch a fish before you can clean it!" Unmarried people living together are part of the harvest, too.

The harvest is ugly. It's young people in mental institutions, jails, and prisons. It's lines of people outside of crack houses as commonplace as grocery store checkout lanes.

The harvest is teen suicide here in our own city. One day I went to see a thirteen-year-old girl named Amy in the intensive care unit at the hospital. "What happened to you?" I asked. She said she'd taken a .38-caliber pistol, put it pointblank to her chest, and pulled the trigger twice. The bullets blasted through her body but somehow didn't kill her.

"Oh, Amy, why, why, why?" I cried.

She said that she was depressed and distraught. Two weeks before, her boyfriend took a sawed-off shotgun, put it in his mouth, and blew his brains out. He was only sixteen.

The harvest is Ben, a sixteen-year-old, all-star high school quarterback I visited in a mental institution. Committed for drugs and a self-destructive lifestyle, Ben shuffled into the room in a hospital gown, spittle drooling down his face. He grabbed me and said, "I'm so scared. I don't want to live this way anymore." A little while later, he somehow managed to get hold of a 9-millimeter pistol and fatally shoot himself.

Oh, Christian, lift up your eyes and see the harvest! This year a million and a half unborn children will be murdered while the church sits by and wants to hear stories about the Rapture. Since 1972, abortion has snuffed out the lives of more than twenty million babies.

The devil is attacking our teens and children with the vile evil of pornography. It has become a multimillion-dollar-a-year business to depict seven-, eight-, nine-, and ten-year-old children having sex with adults. My sources in Washington, D.C., tell me that federal officials are gravely concerned over the increase of so-called "snuff" films that actually show children being killed during the act of sex. These videos are in great demand and sell at premium prices. We live in a society that's gone mad.

This is the harvest—disgusting, sick, and ugly.

No wonder Jesus said, "Lift up your eyes and look, the fields are white already to harvest."

We've been too busy shouting and singing and dancing in the aisles, safe inside the walls of the church. But the harvest is out on the mean streets and in the dark alleys, in the marketplace, the schools, the office complexes, in the inner-city public housing projects, and out in the affluent suburbs. There are no boundaries to sin and degradation, no limits to the suffering, shame, and misery going on all around us every day.

Not long ago, we loaded up about fifteen inner-city kids on a bus and drove them over to Lakeland to a wrestling tournament. While we were there, I received the education of my life. All the kids were having a great time. There were about four thousand of them, on their feet cheering their wrestlers on. Suddenly there was a bright flash of light and a noise like a gun. All the other kids in the arena just cheered louder, but our fifteen inner-city kids hit the floor and ducked under the chairs. Just a freak incident, you say. No, those kids had heard that sound before—been around random shootings often enough that their reflexes just took over and drove them to take cover.

That's the harvest field God has called us to.

You say, "I don't know what I can do to help. I don't have any special talents. I've never had any training to work with troubled people. I can't preach or sing. I'd help if I could, but there's nothing I can do."

A lady named Gwen got involved in our church, and God began doing a great work in her life. She hadn't been to church in almost thirty years, but the love and power of God touched her, restored her, and renewed her faith. So she went to Paula and said, "Is there anything at all I could do to help? I've wasted so much of my life that I don't have much to offer. What can I do, Pastor?"

Paula said, "Can you play jacks?"

"Jacks, Pastor? Well, sure, I guess I still know how to do that."

"Great, that's all you have to do. There are lots of little inner-city kids who are starving for somebody to play with them, show them how to play jacks, talk just to them, and give them a hug. Can you go where they are and just love them a little bit?"

And so she did. Gwen went on an Operation Explosion truck as a helper, with a pocketful of rubber balls and jacks. In ten minutes flat after she sat down and took out her ball and jacks, she had little boys and girls crawling all over her, laughing and squealing, whispering secrets in her ear. They weren't critical of her witness techniques—they were just drawn to her warmth and love.

Gwen sat there on the sidewalk, tears streaming down her face, hugging kids. That one mission trip changed her life. Now she's one of the most effective soul-winning evangelists we've got.

What about you? Can you play jacks? Can you take a boy or girl fishing? Do you like to shoot baskets or toss a football or baseball around? Do it with some kids who don't have a dad. What's your hobby or craft—why not share it with someone who needs help? What if you rounded up a bunch of people less fortunate than yourself and cooked out in your backyard?

Oh no, no, no, we're too busy going to church. We've got to attend another conference on spiritual warfare. We've got to go hear another speaker who specializes in preaching us happy. And all the while, a lost and dying world is going to hell in a hand-basket...and nobody seems to care.

Why don't you take a look at the harvest? Why don't you do something—anything to reach out? See what it feels like to make a difference in somebody's life. You'll have to change your plans. It will take longer than one hour on Sunday morning.

But while you're at it, you just may bump into a quiet man with gentle eyes there at the turnoff to Samaria. You'll know Him when you see Him. You may even hear Him whisper, "Well done."

ABOUT THE AUTHOR

Dr. Randy White is an ordained minister known for his dynamic preaching, exhortation of the Word through illustrated sermons, and his delivery of the Scriptures through practical teaching. He communicates the exciting message of Christ with sincerity and intensity, bringing it down to concrete reality on the issues facing us today.

Randy White is senior pastor of Without Walls International Church, which he cofounded with his wife, Paula, in Tampa, Florida. It was formerly known as South Tampa Christian Center. Without Walls is a thriving, multiracial expression of over four thousand in the Christian community. It has been recognized as one of the fastest-growing churches in the United States, ministering to over ten thousand people weekly. Prior to establishing Without Walls International Church, he pastored several churches with a marked history of phenomenal growth.

Pastor Randy White travels across America and around the world, calling people back to repentance and training pastors and lay leaders how to evangelize their cities and reach the unchurched, the unlovable, the homeless, and the neglected. In his travels he has worked with many world-renowned Christian leaders. He has met with General Colin Powell, former chairman of the Joint Chiefs of Staff, and Margaret Thatcher, former prime minister of Great Britain.

Randy's heartbeat is evangelism and restoration. He has served on the executive committee for the Tampa Crusade of the Billy Graham Evangelistic Association, and he also established a not-for-profit Community Development Corporation (REACT). He creates and produces a daily television program, *Without Walls.* Through his intense outreach vision, Without Walls International Church now hosts 108 satellite churches and ministries, as well as over 200 outreach and in-house ministries.

Pastor White's education in ministerial studies includes attendance at Lee College (now known as Lee University), a bachelor's degree in Bible, a master's degree in divinity, and an honorary doctorate in humane letters.

Ministries of Without Walls International Church

Following is a list of some of the ministries of Without Walls International Church. I hope this list will stir up your desire to be a soulwinner and give you creative and inspirational ideas to reach out beyond the four walls of your church. God is no respecter of persons; the same things we have done for His glory in Tampa, you can do in your church, neighborhood, and city. If we can help or encourage you in any way, please contact our ministry offices at 813-879-HOPE (4673).

Adoption Support Group

AIDS Patient Outreach

Altar Counseling Ministry

Angels of Love (ministry to the terminally ill)

Back-to-School Bash

Balloons Express Love Basket for Kids

Benevolence Ministry

Brochure Creation and Production Ministry

Bus Ministry for Adults and Children

Business Administration Team

Children's Home Orphanage Ministry

Christmas Extravaganza Toy Distribution

Clothes Closet

Club X Teen Center/ "Light" Club

Community Development Corporation (CDC) Seminars

Computers Promoting Unity (CPU) Web Site Ministry

Conquering Force Team

Contracts and Legal Documents Education Ministry

Corporate Evangelism Outreach (CEO) Ministry

Cosmetology Education Ministry

Counseling Ministry

Creators Café and Bookstore

Crossroads Training Center for Women

Custodial Ministry

Davidic Dancing Team

Deliverance Education and Preparation

Ministries of Without Walls

Destiny Academy Christian School

Destiny Bible College

Disaster Relief Ministry

Discipleship Ministry

Distribution Media Scheduling Team

Drag Racing Ministry

English to Spanish Translation Ministry

Entrepreneurship Ministry

Eternal Rhythm (youth dance team)

Event Product Sorting and Distribution

Extreme Praise and Youth Music Team

Financial Counseling Ministry

Focus on Young Individuals (FYI)

Food Pantry and Distribution

For Women Only Bible Study

Foster Care Training Program

GED Program

"Getting Out" Field Trips Outreach Team

Go Tell It Productions (youth drama team)

Graphics/Design Ministry

Greeters Ministry

Grounds Beautification Ministry

Higher Dimensions Education

Hospital Visitation Team

Hospitality for Guest Speakers

Housecleaning Ministry

Illustrative Sermon and Props Team

In-house Printing Ministry

Intercessory Prayer Team

Jr. Kids Explosion Children's Church

KICK (Kids in Christ's Kingdom) Ministry

Kids Alive Summer Camp

Kids Character Ministry

Kids Computer Network

Kids Dance and Drama Team

Kids Explosion

King's Kids

Kingdom Posse Youth Discipleship Training

Ladies' Luncheon Ministry

Liberty Ministries (homosexual community)

Love Baskets

Loyal Warriors Motorcycle Ministry

Man-to-Man Men's Ministries

Marriage Enrichment Seminars

Marriage Ministry and Counseling

Master Pastor Internship Program (MPIP)

Ministries of Without Walls

Masterpiece Ministries (characters and clowns)

Meal Preparation and Delivery Ministry

Media Press Booking and Consultant Ministry

Medical Overseas Missions

Mentoring and Arts Center

Mimes Ministry

Music and Band Ministry

Music Recording Projects

New Converts Ministry

Newcomer Informational Center

NFL Bible Study

Nursery Ministry

Nursing and Convalescent Home Ministry

Offering Counting Team

Office Construction and Engineering Ministry

Operation Explosion (10 teams)

Operation Explosion International Training Center

Operation Med-Care

Operation Rock, Inc.

PTCA (Parents/Teachers Christian Association)

Parking Lot Attendants Ministry

Photography Ministry

Political Action Group

Pregnancy Crisis Center Networking

Prison Ministry

Professional Athletes Ministry

Puppets Ministry

RAW (Rime and Worship Rap Team)

REACT (Restoration and Evangelism Advanced Through Community Training)

Road to Recovery

Seasonal Musical Productions

Security Ministry

Sign Language Ministry

Singles Ministry

Sound and Technicians Ministry

Spanish Youth Outreach Ministry

Special Events and Outings

Student Steering Ministry

TLC (Tender Loving Care) Ministry

Table in the Wilderness Annual Thanksgiving Banquet

Tape Distribution/Production Ministry

Television Commercials Production Ministry

Television Equipment Coordinating Ministry

Ministries of Without Walls

Transportation/Vehicles Maintenance

Tribe Leaders Training (mentoring for women)

R&E Truck Driving School

Ushers Ministry

VISION (job placement)

Vo-Tech/Trade Education

Weddings Coordinating Ministry

Well Care Team

Without Walls Call Center Ministry

Without Walls Correspondence Ministry

Without Walls Partners

Without Walls Television Program Teams

Women of the Word Bible Study

World's Largest Easter Egg Hunt

X-Strippers Support Group

Young at Heart Seniors Ministry

Youth Sports Ministry

Youth With A Mission/Island Breeze International

Three times each year Without Walls International Church hosts an Operation Explosion International Training Center to raise up and equip leaders, laymen, ministers, and pastors on how to organize and operate these ministries. Call 813-879-HOPE, ext. 261, for a free brochure with upcoming dates and information.

If you enjoyed *Without Walls*, here are some other titles from Charisma House that we think will minister to you…

Taking Our Cities for God
John Dawson
ISBN: 0-88419-764-8
Retail Price: $13.99

This book invites you to take part in a spiritual clean-up program that will change you and your community forever! *Taking Our Cities for God* offers a revised and detailed action plan that will open the heavens and allow God's blessings to flow freely.

The Missions Addiction
David Shibley
ISBN: 0-88419-772-7
Retail Price: $13.99

In these action-packed pages, you will discover a Global Jesus Generation that is creating discomfort in the church and change in missions worldwide. God is calling you to become part of a contagious epidemic of missions-hearted believers who will bring global fame to His name!

Bruchko
Bruce Olson
ISBN: 0-88419-133-8
Retail Price: $12.99

What happens when a nineteen-year-old boy leaves home and heads into the jungles to evangelize a murderous tribe of South American Indians? For Bruce Olson it meant capture, disease, terror, loneliness and torture. But what he discovered by trial and error has revolutionized the world of missions. And today the Motilones have become carriers of the gospel and the first native Indians to achieve political status in the history of Colombia.

 **Charisma®** **HOUSE** To pick up a copy of any of these titles, contact your local Christian bookstore or order online at www.charismahouse.com.